CONFIDENTIAL CONFESSIONS

CONFIDENTIAL CONFESSIONS

Volume Two
by Reiko Momochi

Los Angeles • Tokyo • London

Translator - Amy Forsyth
English Adaptation - Marion Brown
Copy Editor - Amy Court Kaemon
Retouch and Lettering - Angie Lee
Cover Artist - Aaron Suhr
Graphic Designer - Deron Bennett

Editor - Julie Taylor
Managing Editor - Jill Freshney
Production Coordinator - Antonio DePietro
Production Manager - Jennifer Miller
Art Director - Matt Alford
Editorial Director - Jeremy Ross
VP of Production - Ron Klamert
President & C.O.O. - John Parker
Publisher & C.E.O. - Stuart Levy

Email: editor@TOKYOPOP.com
Come visit us online at www.TOKYOPOP.com

A  Manga

TOKYOPOP Inc.
5900 Wilshire Blvd. Suite 2000
Los Angeles, CA 90036

ISBN: 1-59182-394-3

First TOKYOPOP® printing: September 2003

10 9 8 7 6 5 4 3 2 1
Printed in the USA

<Contents>

だ

なみ

TEARS

OTOWA
SCHOOL
FOR
GIRLS

SUZUKI! WHAT THE HECK WAS THAT?
HERE HE COMES!
DO I HAVE TO TEACH YOU *EVERYTHING* FROM THE BEGINNING?

Like this!
BEND YOUR KNEES MORE!
ジョリ
ジョリ
DAMN HIM.
TURN YOUR TORSO SIDEWAYS, AND TWIST YOUR ELBOWS THIS WAY.
DON'T PUSH THE BALL... LIFT IT!
ス

GOT IT?
...
....
HEY! DON'T SLACK OFF OVER THERE!
YOU CALL THAT A STRETCH?
LIKE THIS!

THE TENNIS CLUB IS GOING TO BE IN A TOURNAMENT IN AUGUST.
TENNIS CLUB TO PARTICIPATE IN INTER-HIGH COMPETITION!
TWO YEARS AGO, WE GOT FOURTH PLACE. LAST YEAR, WE GOT THIRD. BUT THIS YEAR, WE HAVE A REALLY ENTHUSIASTIC TEAM, AND WE'RE EXPECTING AN EASY WIN.
音羽女子高校
HONESTLY, NO ONE EVER THOUGHT COACH TODO COULD ACTUALLY BRING US THIS FAR.
WE'VE MADE IT INTO THE PRESTIGIOUS INTER-HIGH COMPETITION, EVEN THOUGH NONE OF THE GIRLS EVEN HAVE ANY EXPERIENCE IN THE *JUNIOR* TENNIS CLUB!

WHATEVER HE'S DOING, IT'S CERTAINLY WORKING.
Ding Dong
SPERM CAN SURVIVE FOR ABOUT TWO TO THREE DAYS.
BUT THERE HAVE BEEN CASES OF SPERM MAINTAINING THE ABILITY TO FERTILIZE AFTER MORE THAN THREE DAYS.
Heh heh heh heh
AS A MATTER OF FACT, MINE LIVE FOR SIX DAYS!
TENNIS CLUB COACH SHIGERU TODO, AGE 37 (SINGLE)
HEALTH & PHYSICAL EDUCATION TEACHER

THE BEST WAY TO PREVENT A PREGNANCY IS TO USE A CONDOM.
HOW MANY TIMES IS HE GOING TO TELL US THAT?
THIS ISN'T SEX EDUCATION. IT'S MORE LIKE A BUNCH OF HIS DIRTY STORIES!
SUZUKI! CHIKA SUZUKI, ARE YOU LISTENING?
ARE YOU USING CONTRACEPTION?
DO YOU KNOW HOW TO PUT ON A CONDOM CORRECTLY?
YOU DO USE CONDOMS, DON'T YOU?
HMM? WHAT'S THE MATTER?
....
DON'T TELL ME YOU'RE STILL A VIRGIN?!

HAVEN'T YOU EVER SEEN AN ERECT PENIS?
YOU KNOW, A *PENIS*?
RIGHT?
STOP IT!
STOP IT!

ガコン
YOU SHOULD JUST BRUSH IT OFF LIKE WE DO, CHIKA.
WHY ARE YOU IGNORING IT? WHEN HE'S COACHING THE TENNIS CLUB, HE TOUCHES THE GIRLS IN WAYS THAT JUST AREN'T RIGHT!
HE'S DONE IT TO BOTH OF YOU, TOO.
BRUSH IT OFF?
YOU GUYS HATE IT TOO, DON'T YOU? THOSE LESSONS, THE DISGUSTING WAY HE TALKS, AND ALL THAT...
WELL, I'D RATHER LISTEN TO THAT THAN HAVE A REAL CLASS.
HA HA HA!
I don't know if it was on purpose...
WELL, IT'S NOT LIKE HE CAN AVOID TOUCHING US COMPLETELY IF HE'S GOING TO COACH US, RIGHT? SO THERE'S NOTHING WE CAN DO ABOUT IT.
YOU'RE JUST WORRYING TOO MUCH, CHIKA!
....
Hey! Watch the length of your skirt!
WHAT? HE'S THE DRESS CODE POLICE NOW?
NOW, NOW. WHAT'S THE BIG DEAL?
But...
Oh, great.
Say that louder, Coach Todo!
SCHOOL REGULATIONS NOWADAYS ARE NONSENSE.

LOOK, EVEN THIS LENGTH IS PERFECTLY FINE.
HUH?
OR MAYBE EVEN HIGHER!
Yaaugh!
ばっ
Oh, sorry, sorry, it was an accident
PERVERT! LOSER! I CAN'T BELIEVE HIM!
Ha ha ha!
Now wasn't that more effective?
WORTHLESS OLD MAN. YOU BETTER NOT PUSH YOUR LUCK.
SIGH. ANYWAY, I'M GOING SHOPPING TODAY.
SOUNDS GREAT!
SO HE'S NASTY AND GETS CARRIED AWAY... BUT IS THAT ALL THERE IS TO IT?
THE OTHER GIRLS LETTING HIM GET AWAY WITH IT, JUST LIKE THAT?
AM I REALLY THE ONLY ONE WHO THINKS SOMETHING UNCOOL IS GOING ON HERE?

COULD WHAT HE'S DOING BE WHAT I THINK IT IS?
キーンコーン…
NISHIYAMA'S LEFT LEG STILL HASN'T HEALED, SO I'M AFRAID SHE'S NO LONGER ABLE TO COMPETE.
SO TODAY, WE'RE GOING TO CHOOSE A NEW CAPTAIN.
THANKS FOR YOUR HARD WORK, NISHIYAMA!
HUH? NISHIYAMA!
THE NEW CAPTAIN WILL BE 11TH GRADER CHIKA SUZUKI!
NO ONE HAS ANY OBJECTIONS, RIGHT?
WH...WHAT?
パチパチ
I'M COUNTING ON YOU.
HUH? ME?
WHY ME?
I THINK YOU'D BE GREAT AS THE CAPTAIN!
YOU PUT IN ENOUGH EFFORT FOR TWO OR THREE PEOPLE.

DON'T YOU THINK YOU SHOULD HAVE MORE CONFIDENCE IN YOURSELF, SUZUKI?
COACH TODO APPROVES OF YOU, AFTER ALL.
Hmm...
....
A, ANYWAY...
...THE DAYS RIGHT BEFORE THE COMPETITION ARE IMPORTANT, SO DON'T STIR UP ANY TROUBLE.
AS LONG AS YOU JUST DO WHAT COACH TODO SAYS, NOTHING WILL GO WRONG. OKAY?
OKAY.
Hey! Suzuki! C'mere for a minute!
HURRY UP! I'M IN THE TEACHERS' LOUNGE!
HUH?
COMING!
....
PE TEACHERS' LOUNGE

HUH?
GIVE ME A MASSAGE.
ME?
YEAH. EVERY MUSCLE IN MY BODY IS STIFF. RUB THEM DOWN FOR ME.
WHAT'RE YOU STANDIN' THERE FOR? DIDN'T YOU HEAR ME?

キーンコーン…
AAAH, YEAH. RIGHT THERE.
MMM...THIS FEELS GOOD. YOU'RE BETTER AT THIS THAN NISHIYAMA.
......
WHAT AGE WERE YOU WHEN YOU STARTED PLAYING TENNIS?
OH, I WAS IN 3RD GRADE.
I STARTED PRETTY LATE.
WHAT A WASTE.
YOU COULD PROBABLY EVEN GO TO WIMBLEDON.
DO YOU WANNA TURN PRO RIGHT AFTER YOU GRADUATE?
WIMBLEDON?! ME, A PRO?!
SO NISHIYAM WAS DOIN THIS THE WHOLE TIME?!
HUH? PRO?
I DON'T THINK I'M THAT GOOD YET...
DON'T TELL ME YOU'RE SATISFIED WITH JUST BEING IN THE INTER-HIGH?
I'M NOT GOING TO TWIST YOUR ARM, BUT YOU HAVE PERFECT TIMING WHEN YOU RETURN A SERVE. YOU'D BE LETTING ALL THAT TALENT GO TO WASTE.

SOME OF YOUR SHOTS REMIND ME OF KIMIKO DATE.*
*KIMIKO DATE WAS A FAMOUS JAPANESE TENNIS PLAYER. SHE IS NOW RETIRED.
BUT KIMIKO HAD SOMETHING YOU DON'T... SHE HAD WILLPOWER.
YOU HAVE TO MATCH HER WILLPOWER, TECHNIQUE, AND STRENGTH.
WILLPOWER?
WHEN YOU'RE UNDER PRESSURE, YOU THINK YOU'RE GOING TO LOSE, AND THEN YOU LOSE YOUR CONFIDENCE.
ドキッ
IT HAPPENED WHEN YOU HAD YOUR FIRST MATCH LAST YEAR.
AND WHEN YOU'RE ON THE COURT...
HE SEES RIGHT THROUGH ME!

"COACH TODO APPROVES OF YOU, AFTER ALL."
I WONDER IF I MISUNDERSTOOD HIM.
AND BESIDES, SOME OF THE OTHER GIRLS SAY THEY LIKE TODO BECAUSE HE'S EASY TO TALK TO ABOUT SEX.
I WAS PROBABLY JUST NERVOUS AND OVERLY SENSITIVE.
CAN YOU SHOW ME THAT, SOME DAY, YOU'LL BE READY TO STAND ON THE COURT IN FRONT OF THE WORLD?
GOT IT?
HUH?
......
Y...YES, SIR.
HEY, GET ON TOP OF ME.
HUH?
YOU CAN PUT MORE STRENGTH INTO THE MASSAGE THAT WAY.
じろっ
O... OKAY...
I GUESS YOU'RE RIGHT.

......
ドキドキドキ
IS THIS... OKAY?
MMM... JUST PERFECT!

7月
Kimiko Date
Date

THAT WAS SO FAST!
7TH GRADE
KIMIKO DATE COULD RETURN THE BALL SO FAST, HER OPPONENTS DIDN'T HAVE TIME TO RESPOND. AND HER SHOTS WERE LOW, MAKING THEM EVEN HARDER TO RETURN.
AND LOW!
HER FAST RISING STROKE SCARED EVEN THE TOP PLAYERS.

SHE EVEN DEFEATED THE TOP-RANKED PLAYER IN THE WORLD, STEFFI GRAF.
SHE TAUGHT ME THAT BEING SMALL ISN'T A HANDICAP AT ALL.

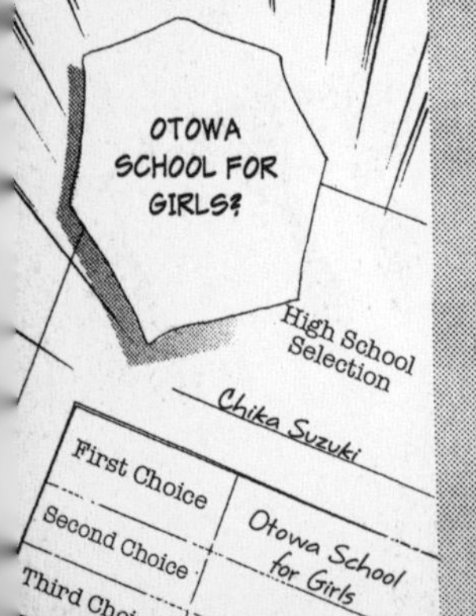
OTOWA SCHOOL FOR GIRLS?
High School Selection
Chika Suzuki
First Choice
Otowa School for Girls
Second Choice
Third Choice

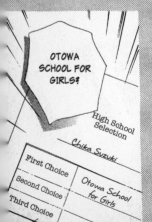

Why THIS school?

IT WOULD TAKE AN HOUR TO COMMUTE THERE.

YOU DIDN'T PICK IT BECAUSE THE UNIFORMS LOOK CUTE, DID YOU?

I WANT TO PLAY TENNIS AT OTOWA.

I HAVE TO GO TO OTOWA! PLEASE!

YOU CAN PLAY TENNIS AT ANY SCHOOL!

High School Entrance Exam

uide To Famous Private Girls' High Schools

"THE FAMOUS COACH WHO TOOK A BUNCH OF AVERAGE, ROOKIE STUDENTS AND TURNED THEM INTO TOP PLAYERS IN A SHORT TIME." COACH TODO'S NAME SHOWED UP IN ALMOST EVERY BOOK I READ.

Tennis Coach

* Coach Shigeru Todo "Everyone has some undiscovered talent..."

Coach Todo's 7th straight Inter-High team. Coach Todo's training methods are tough, but...

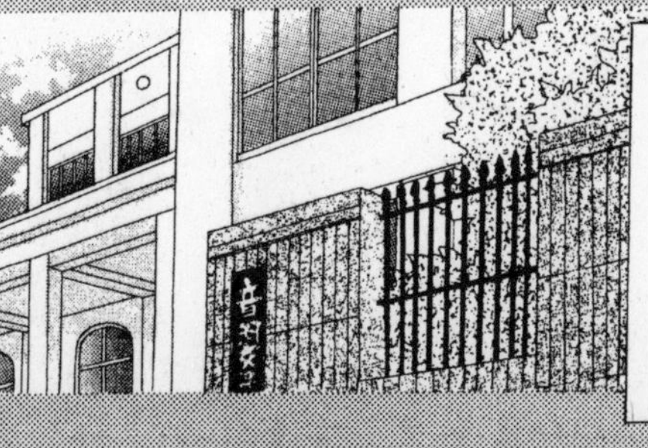

I THOUGHT IF I WENT TO THIS SCHOOL, EVEN I COULD BE IN THE INTER-HIGH.
IT WAS MY DREAM.

WE LOOK FORWARD TO BEING COACHED BY YOU.
I BELIEVED THAT AS LONG I HAD THIS COACH, I COULD DO IT.
AS LONG AS I HAD THIS COACH...
THAT'S RIGHT...
HE'S THE COACH.
I'M A MEMBER OF HIS TEAM.
THIS IS JUST A SIMPLE MASSAGE.
I CAN'T CAUSE ANY TROUBLE...

AWESOME RELAY!
IT'S LIKE SHE'S IN A MATCH.
SHE'S ALMOST SCARY TODAY!
OH, NO..!
SHE'S GONNA HIT THE...
CRASH
CHIKA!
WHAT DID YOU HIT? YOUR CHEST?
YEAH, BUT I'M FINE.

THAT WAS A SHOCK.
ALL RIGHT! THAT'S IT FOR TODAY!
SUZUKI, COME WITH ME FOR A MOMENT.
PE Teachers' Lounge
WHAT?
TAKE OFF YOUR CLOTHES.
YOU TOOK A REALLY BAD SPILL. I JUST NEED TO SEE IF YOU'RE HURT.
I'M...I'M FINE. REALLY.
Y...YES, SIR.
YOU MIGHT HAVE FRACTURED ONE OF YOUR BONES.
IT'S NO BIG DEAL. JUST HURRY UP AND TAKE OFF YOUR CLOTHES.

ドキドキ

THERE'S NO REASON TO BLUSH.

じろじろ

プチッ

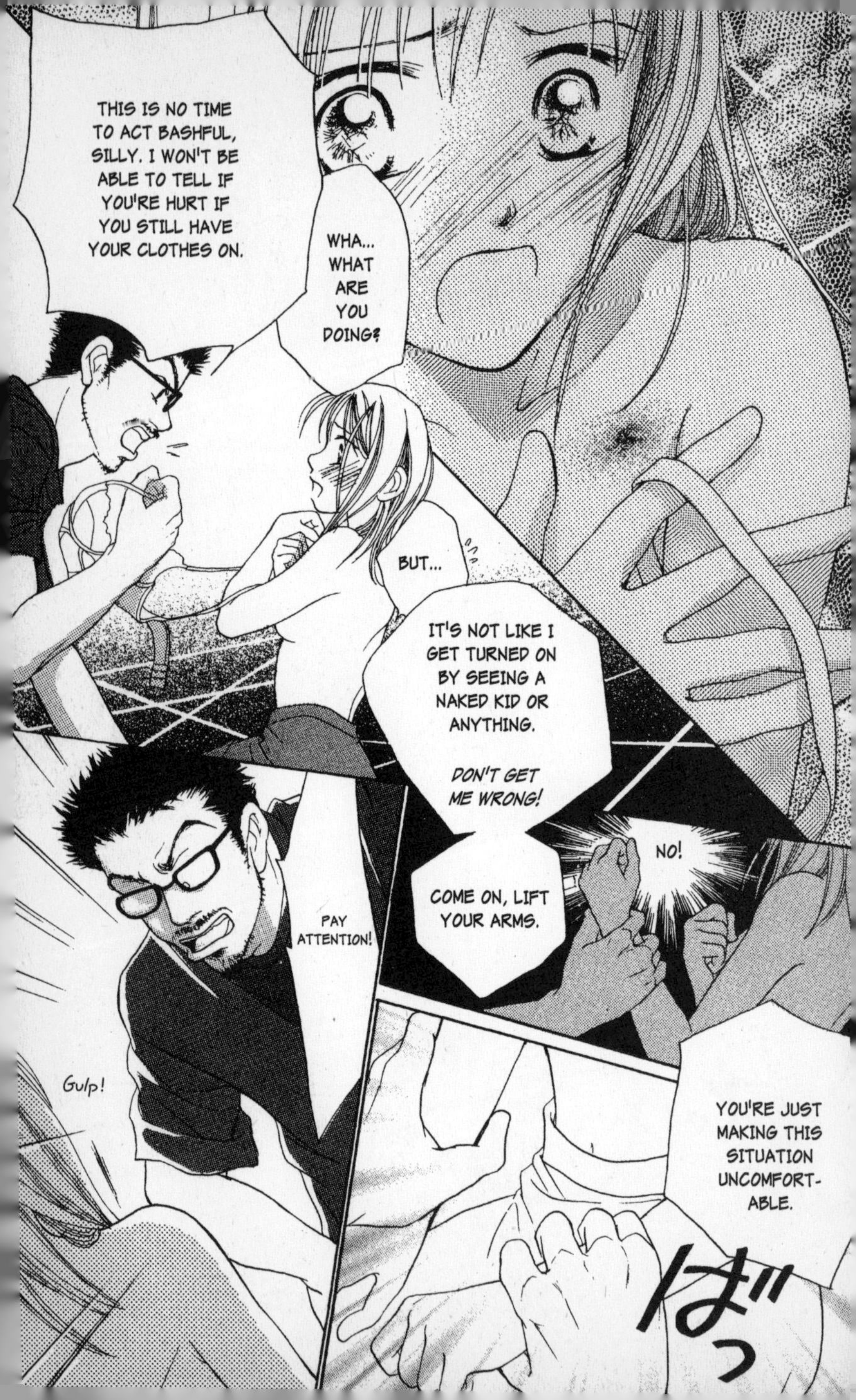
WHA... WHAT ARE YOU DOING?
THIS IS NO TIME TO ACT BASHFUL, SILLY. I WON'T BE ABLE TO TELL IF YOU'RE HURT IF YOU STILL HAVE YOUR CLOTHES ON.
BUT...
IT'S NOT LIKE I GET TURNED ON BY SEEING A NAKED KID OR ANYTHING.
DON'T GET ME WRONG!
PAY ATTENTION!
Gulp!
NO!
COME ON, LIFT YOUR ARMS.
YOU'RE JUST MAKING THIS SITUATION UNCOMFORT-ABLE.
ばっ

DOES IT HURT HERE?
Y...YES, SIR.
WHAT ABOUT HERE?
NO.
HERE?
A LITTLE.
I SEE... SO IT HURTS WHEN I PRESS YOUR RIB UNDERNEATH YOUR PECTORAL MUSCLE.
HMM...
OH, NO... HE'S TOUCHING LOWER AND LOWER.
ちら
I'LL TRY PRESSING A LITTLE LOWER THEN...

NO!
BAM BAM
COACH TODO, ARE YOU IN THERE?
I CAME FOR THOSE RECORDS...
TH-TH-THEY'RE OVER THERE.
YOU JUST NEEDED THE RECORDS FOR THIS YEAR, RIGHT?
UM...
UH, YEAH...
SUZUKI, YOU DON'T SEEM TO HAVE FRACTURED ANY BONES, SO YOU CAN GO HOME NOW.

ギュッ…

IF THAT GUY HADN'T SHOWN UP, THE COACH WOULD'VE TOUCHED ME EVEN FARTHER DOWN.

BUT HE WAS JUST MAKING SURE I WASN'T HURT.

HE'S A P.E. TEACHER AND MY COACH, AFTER ALL...

I'M SURE IT'S NOT THAT STRANGE.

"YOU'RE WORRYING TOO MUCH ABOUT IT, CHIKA."

"IT'S NOT LIKE HE CAN AVOID TOUCHING US COMPLETELY IF HE'S GOING TO COACH US."

BUT...

ばっ…
ハァハァハァ
……

I'M FINISHED.
HUH? BUT YOU HARDLY ATE ANYTHING, CHIKA.
WHAT'S WRONG? YOU HAVEN'T BEEN EATING MUCH LATELY EITHER.
SHE'S PROBABLY JUST NERVOUS.
I WONDER IF I SHOULD QUIT SCHOOL... BUT THEN I'D HAVE TO QUIT TENNIS, TOO.
TENNIS

SHE'S BEEN DREAMING ABOUT BEING IN THE INTER-HIGH, AND NOW THAT DREAM'S ABOUT TO COME TRUE. I'D BE NERVOUS, TOO.
AND SHE'S THE TEAM CAPTAIN NOW, SO SHE HAS MORE RESPONSIBILITY.
BUT YOU NEED TO TAKE IT EASY ONCE IN A WHILE, ALSO, CHIKA.
IF YOU'RE TOO SERIOUS AND TENSE, IT'S NOT GOOD FOR YOUR BODY.
COME ON! TAKE A DEEP BREATH. RELAX, OKAY?
EVEN IF I TELL SOMEONE ABOUT TODO, THEY'D PROBABLY JUST THINK I WAS OVERREACTING...
SEE YOU LATER.
DID SOMETHING HAPPEN AT SCHOOL?
CHIKA...
I WONDER WHAT MOM WOULD THINK...

UM...
UMM, WELL, COACH TODO...
...IN THE TEACHERS' LOUNGE, HE...
....
YOU CAN TELL ME, CHIKA.
....
HE TOLD ME I COULD BE A PRO.
HEH HEH.
SEE YOU LATER.
I CAN'T TELL HER!

I JUST CAN'T TELL HER!
Good morning!
ALMOST TIME FOR CLASS!
ぱし
COME ON! YOU'RE LATE!
YAAAH!
Hurry up!
Aaugh!
You better run for the classroom.
Ha ha ha!

HEY YAMAMOTO, WHY DO YOU HAVE BLACK RINGS UNDER YOUR EYES?
DID YOU HAVE SEX WITH YOUR BOYFRIEND AGAIN LAST NIGHT?
N...NO!
THEN DID YOU MASTURBATE TOO MUCH?
Ha ha ha ha ha!
I HATE TODO.
I'M GOING TO COME IN THROUGH THE BACK GATE FROM NOW ON.
ISN'T I LOCKED
I CAN JUST CLIMB OVER IT. THAT'S BETTER THAN GETTING TOUCHED BY HIM.
?
SO I'M NOT THE ONLY ONE SUFFERING.
YOU'RE LATE, TOO, SUZUKI.

HMM, YOU LOOK PALE.
?
?
?
HAVING YOUR PERIOD, HUH?
I WANTED TO SAY SOMETHING, BUT COULDN'T...
THE THINGS HE SAYS, THE UNNECESSARY TOUCHING...
ISN'T WHAT HE'S DOING SEXUAL HARASSMENT?

HE SEXUALLY HARASSES HIS STUDENTS.
WE'RE BEING SEXUALLY HARASSED AT SCHOOL!

JULY 10: LEAVING FOR TRAINING CAMP
Softy
34 Maxi-Pads
TAKE IT ALL OUT. ALL OF IT.
YOU STILL HAVE MORE, RIGHT?
......
OH! WHAT DO WE HAVE HERE?
Ya ha ha ha ha!
ITO'S AN F CUP!
No!
!
JUST LOOKIN' AT BRAS DOESN'T TURN ME ON AT ALL, EVEN IF THEY ARE BIG.
THEY TURN ME ON EVEN LESS THAN UNDIES.
HUH? TANAKA'S HAVING HER PERIOD, TOO?
I DIDN'T HEAR ABOUT THAT.
IS ANYONE ELSE HAVING HER PERIOD?
COACH!
SUZUKI, PASS THIS AROUND TO EVERYONE.

!!
DAYS WHEN YOU HAVE YOUR PERIOD
NAME
WH...WHAT IN THE WORLD?
THERE'S NO REASON FOR THIS.
KUNIYASU!
I'M NOT DOIN' IT. THIS IS JUST ONE OF YOUR LITTLE HOBBIES.
THE ONLY REASON YOU'RE CHECKING WHAT WE'RE BRINGING WITH US IS SO YOU CAN SEE OUR UNDERWEAR.
WHAT DID YOU SAY?
ザワザワ
バサ
HEY SUZUKI, YOU REMEMBER WHAT HAPPENED DURING TRAINING CAMP LAST YEAR, RIGHT?

SOMEONE HID CIGARETTES IN HER UNDERWEAR.
AND ANOTHER GIRL LOST A MATCH BECAUSE SHE WAS HAVING HER PERIOD, RIGHT?
......
LISTEN UP! WE'RE GOING FOR SOME SERIOUS TRAINING! WE'RE NOT GOING TO GET SECOND OR THIRD PLACE THIS YEAR, WE'RE GOING TO WIN!
AND WE CAN'T DO THAT UNLESS YOU HAVE THE WILLPOWER, SKILLS, AND STRENGTH!
GOT IT? I'M BETTING EVERYTHING ON THIS TRAINING CAMP, SO WE CAN WIN THE INTER-HIGH!
ANYONE WHO DOESN'T LIKE MY METHODS CAN JUST QUIT RIGHT NOW!

DEAD SILENCE
......
YOU GIRLS ARE DIFFERENT FROM THE WIMPS AT THOSE OTHER SCHOOLS.
RIGHT?
NONE OF YOU HAVE ANY COMPLAINTS ABOUT MY METHODS, RIGHT?
......
......
NO, SIR...
NO, SIR...
NO, SIR...
NO, SIR...
YOU DON'T HAVE ANY COMPLAINTS, RIGHT, SUZUKI?
....

WHAT HE SAID ABOUT LAST YEAR WAS TRUE.
AND THERE'S NOTHING WRONG WITH WHAT HE SAID AS A COACH.
BUT...
......
NO, SIR...
ALL RIGHT! NO FOOLIN' AROUND! EVERYONE WRITE DOWN THE DAYS YOU GET YOUR PERIOD!
WHAT'S GOING ON WITH THIS TEAM?
ARE YOU REALLY OKAY WITH THIS, CAPTAIN?

......
SALLY KUNIYASU. SHE'S IN THE SAME GRADE AS ME. SHE TRANSFERRED HERE IN APRIL WHEN SHE CAME BACK TO JAPAN.
SHE HOLDS THE KEY TO WINNING THE INTER-HIGH.
IN AMERICA, SHE WENT TOE-TO-TOE WITH THE TOP-RANKED JUNIOR PLAYERS IN THE WORLD.
SHE STILL HASN'T GONE TO MANY CHAMPIONSHIP MATCHES YET IN THE THREE MONTHS SINCE SHE'S BEEN BACK. ALL THE SCHOOLS WANT HER ON THEIR TEAM, BUT SHE HASN'T SETTLED ON WHICH ONE SHE REALLY WANTS TO PLAY FOR. SHE'S A TOUGH GIRL.
OTOWA SCHOOL FOR GIRLS TENNIS CLUB TRAINING CAMP

ガラッ

COME ON! HURRY IT UP!

CHIKA!
パク…
A WHOLE WEEK LEFT...
I HAVE TO STAY UNDER THE SAME ROOF AS TODO FOR A WHOLE WEEK...
クチャクチャ

BEER
Buwahaha!
プハー
He did this last year, too.
LADIES RO

GOTTA TAKE A LEAK!
WHAT THE...
COACH, THE GUYS' BATHROOM IS NEXT DOOR!
SHUT UP! IT'S BROKEN. I CAN'T USE IT.
EEEEEEK!
EEEK!
OH NO! THAT'S WHERE I JUST WAS!
PHEEEW! THIS PLACE REEKS!
WHO WAS JUST IN HERE? SAKURAI? WAHAHAHA!
....
SAKURAI!

HEEEY! OPEN UP!
WHAT IS IT?
UH, NAKAHASHI, C'MERE FOR A MINUTE.
HUH?
OVER HERE, OVER HERE.
DON'T WORRY ABOUT IT! JUST GO ON IN.
TODO'S ROOM?
MMM...RIGHT THERE.
YOU'RE EVEN BETTER AT THIS THAN SUZUKI.
HEY, GET ON TOP OF ME. YOU CAN PUT MORE STRENGTH INTO IT THAT WAY.
UMM...
LIKE THIS?
THAT'S WHAT HE SAID TO ME!

HOW MANY STUDENTS ARE YOU GOING TO DO THIS TO?
TODO...!!

2年
DOES IT HURT, SAKURAI?
YEAH...
WHAT DO WE DO? WE DON'T HAVE ANY MEDICINE FOR THIS.
DO YOU WANT TO TRY GOING TO THE BATHROOM AGAIN?
SAKURAI...
UGH...
DON'T PUSH YOURSELF! ACTUALLY, I HAVE MINE, TOO.
BUT TODO'S ALWAYS GOING INTO THE GIRLS' BATHROOM.
Oh— me, too.
IF ONLY HE WAS A FEMALE, THEN HE'D UNDERSTAND.
YOU ONLY HAVE TO HANG IN THERE FOR FOUR MORE DAYS, SAKURAI...

HEEY! EXCUSE ME!
ONE OF YOU, COME TO MY OFFICE.
......
I WONDER WHO IT IS TODAY?
THE OTHER DAY I HAD TO TWEEZE HIS GRAY HAIRS.
YESTERDAY, I HAD TO GIVE HIM A MASSAGE.
WHO'S IT GOING TO BE TODAY?
HOW ABOUT ROCK-PAPER-SCISSORS?
1, 2, 3, shoot!
It's Aiko.
GEEEEH. ME?
ICK.
BYE!
Good luck!
EEEEW...
IT'S LIKE HE THINKS HE'S THE KING.
TELL ME ABOUT IT!
AHAHA!
YOU DON'T HAVE TO GO.
YOU SHOULDN'T HAVE TO GO.

HUH?
BUT...
HIS LITTLE GAMES AREN'T FUNNY.
THIS IS NO JOKE.
WHY IS GETTING CHANGED IN FRONT OF HIM A PART OF TRAINING?
WHY DOES HE MAKE US MASSAGE HIM AND PULL OUT HIS GRAY HAIRS?
WE SHOULD BE FURIOUS!
OF COURSE, EVERYONE'S SICK OF HOW LEWD HE IS.
HE DOESN'T HAVE A SHRED OF DECENCY.
WHAT TODO IS DOING...
I THINK IT'S MORE THAN HIM JUST BEING LEWD, THOUGH.

WHAT TODO IS DOING IS SEXUAL HARASSMENT! IT'S A VIOLATION OF OUR RIGHTS!
WE'RE THE VICTIMS OF SEXUAL HARASSMENT!
DEAD SILENCE
....
SEXUAL HARASSMENT?
YEAH.
IT'S WHEN A GUY MAKES UNWANTED SEXUAL REMARKS OR ADVANCES AT YOU.
WHAT ARE THEY DOING? I TOLD THEM TO COME, DIDN'T I?

HEY! I NEED SOMEONE TO HELP ME WITH THIS COMPRESS!
CAFETERIA
ARE YOUR MUSCLES CRAMPING UP? WHY DON'T I HELP YOU WITH IT?
UM... NO...
IT'S NO BOTHER.
HUH? COACH! COACH!
....
ザワ
THAT'S WHAT I'VE BEEN TRYING TO TELL YOU. HE ALWAYS HAS SOME ULTERIOR MOTIVE.
YOU'RE RIGHT.
HE'S ABUSING HIS AUTHORITY.
ザワ
I MEAN, HAVEN'T THERE BEEN A LOT OF TIMES WHEN HE TOUCHED YOU WHEN HE DIDN'T NEED TO?
YEAH, NOW THAT YOU MENTION IT...
WHEN I LOOK BACK ON IT NOW, I THINK YOU'RE RIGHT...
ザワ
ザワ

EVERYONE...
When we're stretching, he touches me like this.
You're right!
He does this to me.
Why didn't you tell anyone before?
Huh? What's up with that?
But...
THIS MIGHT BE THE SAME AS WHAT YOU'RE TALKING ABOUT... I THINK...
WHEN WE WERE STRETCHING AND COACH TODO WAS PUSHING MY HIPS...
...HE SAID MY PANTS WERE IN THE WAY, AND HE PUSHED THEM DOWN UNTIL HE COULD SEE MY UNDERWEAR...
BUT...
Huh?
IDIOT! HE TRICKED YOU!
DIDN'T YOU REALIZE IT WAS STRANGE?

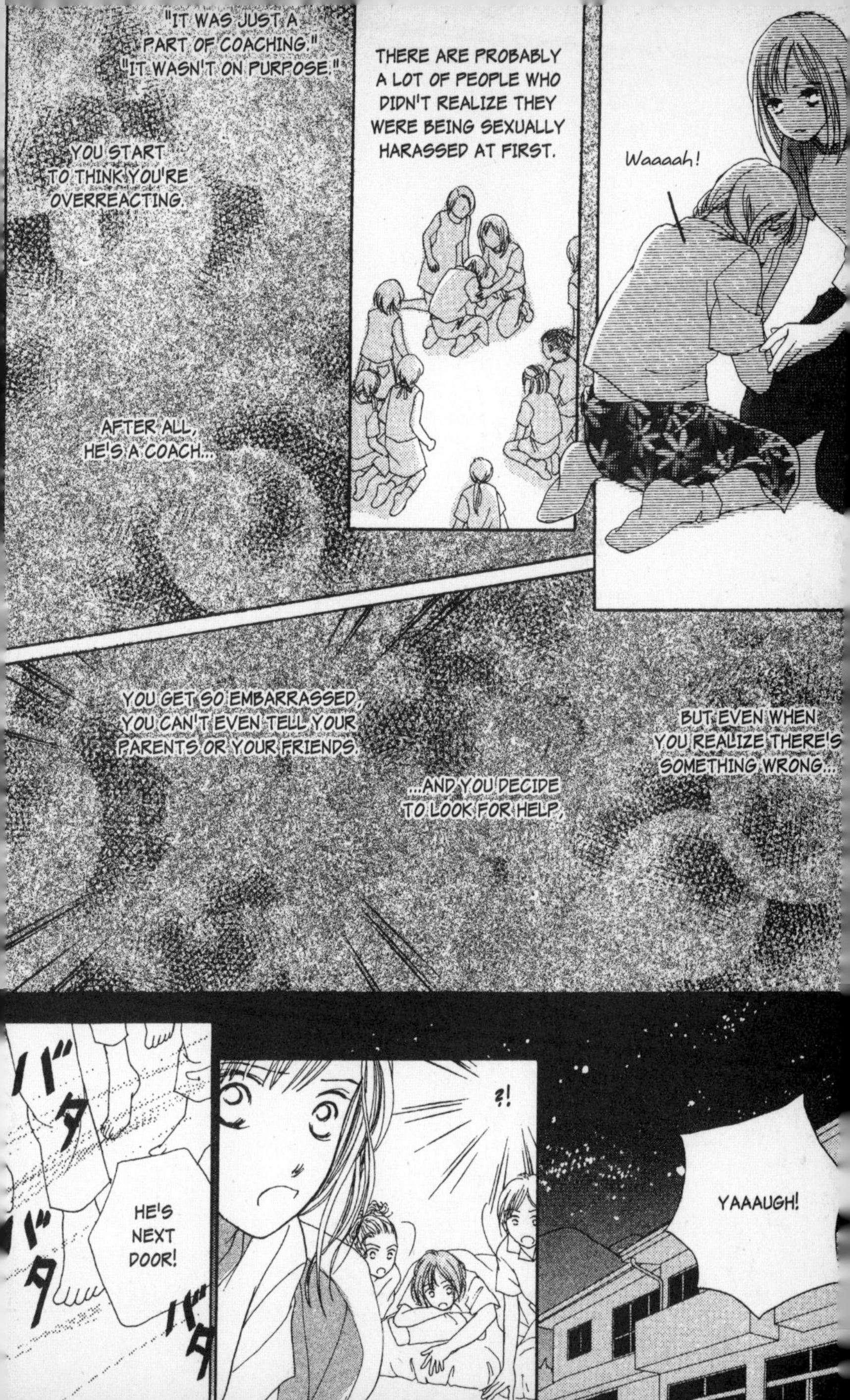
Waaaah!
THERE ARE PROBABLY A LOT OF PEOPLE WHO DIDN'T REALIZE THEY WERE BEING SEXUALLY HARASSED AT FIRST.
"IT WAS JUST A PART OF COACHING." "IT WASN'T ON PURPOSE."
YOU START TO THINK YOU'RE OVERREACTING.
AFTER ALL, HE'S A COACH...
BUT EVEN WHEN YOU REALIZE THERE'S SOMETHING WRONG...
...AND YOU DECIDE TO LOOK FOR HELP,
YOU GET SO EMBARRASSED, YOU CAN'T EVEN TELL YOUR PARENTS OR YOUR FRIENDS.
YAAAUGH!
?!
HE'S NEXT DOOR!
バタ
バタ
バタ

んがー
んごー
HE JUST GOT INTO MY BED!
HE'S DRUNK.
HEY! WAKE UP!
PLEASE, WAKE UP!
DOES HE THINK WE'RE HIS HAREM OR SOMETHING?
んがー ごー〜

スコーン

んががが

WE DON'T HAVE TO TAKE THIS!

ミーン
ミーン
ミーン…
OTOWA SCHOOL FOR GIRLS TENNIS CLUB TRAINING CAMP

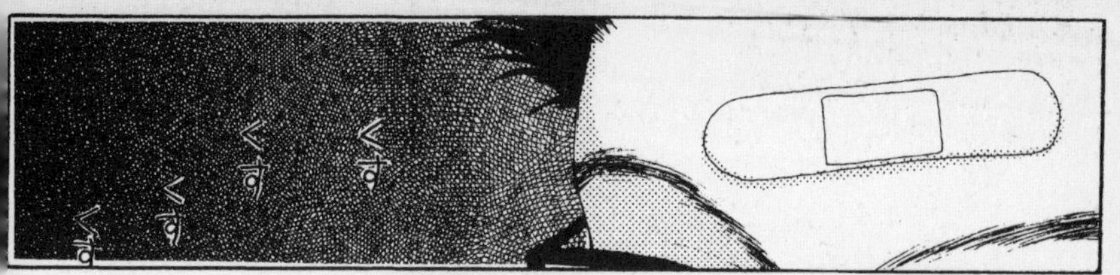
くす くす くす くす

?
TOUCHING US PLACES WHERE IT ISN'T NECESSARY... OBSCENE REMARKS... WE'RE NOT GOING TO TAKE TODO'S SEXUAL HARASSMENT ANYMORE!

SUZUKI! HOW MANY TIMES DO I HAVE TO TELL YOU!
HERE IT COMES.

FIX YOUR KNEES!
LIKE THIS!
ス
ばっ
I'M GETTING CHANGED.
......
HE'S COMING THIS WAY!
OGAWA! YOU CALL THAT A STRETCH?

WHA...WHAT ARE YOU DOING? MOVE YOUR HAND!
NO...
ぐいぐい
パコーン
......
......

INTER-HIGH TEAM MEMBERS
DOUBLES: EMI MATSUNO
ERIKO OGAWA
SINGLES: SALLY KUNIYASU
CHIKA SUZUKI
SALLY KUNIYA
CHIKA SUZU
WHAT?
LISTEN UP!
THIS FINAL SELECTION WILL BE MADE AFTER THE TRAINING CAMP.
CHIKA S

YOU ALL KNOW WHY ALL CLUB MEMBERS HAVE TO GO TO THIS TRAINING CAMP, RIGHT?
IT'S SO EVERYONE CAN HAVE A CHANCE!
YAMAMOTO, YOU'VE MANAGED TO MASTER CONTROL AND WIDEN YOUR RANGE OF PLAY! IT'D BE A WASTE TO KEEP YOU AS THE ALTERNATE.
AND YOU'VE HAVE THE MOST STAMINA ON THE TEAM!
YOU TWO COULD BE THE DARK HORSES OF THE COMPETITION!
ザワ ザワ
ザワ
AND AS FOR YOU, SUZUKI, YOU SEEM TO BE OFF YOUR GAME.
SO IT'S COME TO THIS...

HEEEY! SOMEONE, COME TO MY ROOM!

Hmm, I wonder who will come today...

GEH. SO IT'S *THAT* TODAY.

NO ONE'S GONNA COME ANYMORE.

IDIOT.

YA...YAMAMOTO?

ザワザワ
YOU CAN'T BE SERIOUS. YOU'RE GOING?
BUT...
YAMAMOTO.
ドスドス
BUT I WANTED TO GO!
ぐっ
WE'RE SENIORS, AND IT'S THE LAST CHANCE FOR US TO GO TO THE INTER-HIGH!
CLEANING HIS EARS ISN'T GOING TO MAKE HIM PICK YOU FOR THE INTER-HIGH.
YOU DON'T KNOW THAT FOR SURE!
BUT...
PLAYERS AREN'T PICKED BASED JUST ON HOW GOOD THEY ARE OR HOW MUCH EXPERIENCE THEY HAVE.
THE RELATIONSHIP OF MUTUAL TRUST YOU HAVE WITH THE COACH IS MORE IMPORTANT THAN ANY OF THOSE THINGS.

RELATIONSHIP OF MUTUAL TRUST?
IS THAT WHAT YOU CALL BEING SEXUALLY HARASSED?
YOU SEE EVERYTHING THAT COACH DOES IN A DISTORTED WAY. THAT'S WHY EVEN SIMPLE, NONCHALANT THINGS SEEM OFFENSIVE TO YOU.
Yama
ダッ
コンコン
EXCUSE ME.
パタン
......
......
......
ザワ ザワ
ヒソ ヒソ
6:00
EMERGENCY MEETING

TA-DA!
GUESS WHAT THESE ARE? THE OTOWA SCHOOL FOR GIRLS TENNIS CLUB'S NEW UNIFORMS!
Ha ha!
Reobok
JUST LIKE THE ONES WORN BY SERENA AND VENUS WILLIAMS! YOU'VE ALL SEEN THEM ON TV, RIGHT?
AND LOOK! DOESN'T THIS PINK ONE LOOK GREAT?
That one's just like one I saw someone wear in the Olympics!
ザワ
ザワ
ICK! THOSE THINGS ARE WAY TOO REVEALING!
THAT'S RIGHT! THESE ARE DESIGNED SO YOU DON'T NEED TO WEAR A BRA! FIVE OF YOU TRY THESE ON FOR ME.
DECIDE AMONGST YOURSELVES WHO'S GOING TO WEAR WHICH ONE.

GO AHEAD! ANYONE CAN TRY THEM ON.
ヒソ
ヒソ
FIVE PEOPLE... THAT'S THE SAME NUMBER OF PLAYERS ON THE INTER-HIGH TEAM.
!!
EMI? ERIKO?
I'D REGRET IT FOR THE REST OF MY LIFE IF I WAS LEFT OUT OF THE INTER-HIGH OVER SOMETHING LIKE THIS.
GLAD I GOT ONE.
AND BESIDES, CAMP IS GOING TO BE OVER TOMORROW. I DON'T WANT TO DO ANYTHING TO MESS UP MY CHANCES OF BEING PICKED.
WHAT ARE YOU SAYING?
WHAT'S HAPPENING TO EVERYONE?

ALL RIGHT. LINE UP OVER THERE.

Ooooh, nice!

......

I'd hate to wear those things!

HOW DO YOU LIKE THEM? DON'T THOSE FEEL BETTER THAN THOSE BLAND OUTFITS YOU USED TO WEAR?

AND LOOK! THEY MAKE YOUR CHEST STAND OUT MORE!

Reobok
EVERYONE...

All right! I'm going to make my decision! Good work, ladies!
C...COACH...
YEAH?
Um...
I DON'T THINK WE SHOULD BE WEARING SUCH REVEALING OUTFITS.
HUH?
WHY NOT? THEY LOOK GOOD!
I HAVE TO TELL HIM, AS CAPTAIN OF THE TEAM.
WELL, THE UNIFORMS AREN'T THE ONLY PROBLEM. IT'S ALSO YOUR WAY OF DOING THINGS.
AAH, I SEE, I SEE.
WELL, WE CAN TALK ABOUT THIS LATER.
LATER?
HMM... LET'S SEE...
COME TO MY ROOM TONIGHT AT 10:00.
!!
CAN'T WE TALK SOMEWHERE ELSE?
......
ALL RIGHT, HOW ABOUT OVER THERE?

OKAY.
TODO HASN'T ASKED ANYONE TO COME TO HIS ROOM YET TONIGHT.
HE'S HAD US GIVE HIM A MASSAGE, PULL OUT HIS GRAY HAIRS, CLEAN OUT HIS EARS...
I'M SURE IF WE TALK THINGS OUT, HE'LL UNDERSTAND.
I WAS AFRAID OF WHAT HE WAS GOING TO COME UP WITH FOR THIS LAST NIGHT AT CAMP.
HUH? WHERE'S CHIKA?
HEY! SUZUKI! OVER HERE!
?
OVER WHERE?

IN HERE?
HUH?
WASH MY BACK FOR ME.

I...I CAN'T DO SOMETHING LIKE THAT!
ばっ
HEY, HEY. IF YOU CAN'T DO THIS, THEN HOW CAN YOU WIN AT THE TENNIS MATCH?
WHAT DOES THIS HAVE TO DO WITH TENNIS?
THERE'S A REASON FOR EVERYTHING I MAKE YOU DO.
I'M LEAVING!
DIDN'T YOU HAVE SOMETHING TO TALK TO ME ABOUT?

I'M ALWAYS THE MOST RELAXED WHEN I'M IN THE BATHROOM.
THAT'S WHY I BRING THE CAPTAIN HERE TO HAVE A SERIOUS TALK ABOUT THE CLUB EVERY YEAR.
THAT MIGHT BE THE WAY YOU DO THINGS, BUT...
BUT...
NOT A SINGLE PERSON HAS COMPLAINED.
WELL, WHATEVER.
I DON'T WANT TO FORCE A STUDENT TO DO SOMETHING SHE FEELS UNCOMFORTABLE DOING.
YOU CAN GO BACK TO YOUR ROOM, SUZUKI.
I GUESS I'LL NEVER BE ABLE TO HAVE A SERIOUS TALK WITH YOU, SUZUKI. WHAT A SHAME.
....

WHAT'S WRONG? YOU CAN GO BACK TO YOUR ROOM.
....
PLAYERS AREN'T PICKED BASED JUST ON HOW GOOD THEY ARE OR HOW MUCH EXPERIENCE THEY HAVE.
I'D REGRET IT FOR THE REST OF MY LIFE IF I WAS LEFT OUT OF THE INTER-HIGH OVER SOME-THING LIKE THIS.
REGRET...

AAAH, THAT FEELS GOOD.
RUB HARDER.
ゴシ
ゴシ

HE'S NOT JUST SOME LECHEROUS TEACHER.
HE'S THE FAMOUS COACH WHO BROUGHT THE OTOWA SCHOOL FOR GIRLS TENNIS CLUB TO THE NATIONAL LEVEL.
MAYBE HE'S A PHYSICAL KIND OF PERSON BECAUSE HE WAS BROUGHT UP IN AN ALL-BOYS SCHOOL.
MAYBE THAT'S WHY HE TALKS AND ACTS LIKE THAT.
WELL, YOU SEE, YOU'VE BEEN MAKING STUDENTS GIVE YOU MASSAGES AND WASH YOUR BACK...
...BUT EVERYONE HATES IT.
HUH?
REALLY? DID ALL OF THEM THEY REALLY SAY THAT TO YOU?
AND IT'S NOT JUST THE THINGS YOU DO AT CAMP. IT'S WHAT YOU DO AT REGULAR PRACTICES, TOO.
HMMM... I SEE.
Chuckle
SO YOU DON'T WANT ME TO MAKE ANYONE BUT YOU DO THOSE THINGS, IS THAT RIGHT SUZUKI?
IS THAT IT?
Ha ha! I get it now.
THAT'S NOT WHAT I...
OWO-WOW!

I'M JUST SAYING I WANT YOU TO THINK ABOUT THE GIRLS' FEELINGS. LIKE WITH THOSE OUTFITS...
OOH, THOSE... YOU'RE RIGHT, I DIDN'T GET THE PRINCIPAL'S APPROVAL...
HA HA!
!!
THEN WHY DID YOU HAVE US TRY THEM ON?
THANK YOU! THAT'S ENOUGH.
Aaah, that felt good!
DAMN HIM.
EXCUSE ME! I'M LEAVING!
HEY! WATCH OUT FOR THAT RAZOR!
OH, WHOOPS.

ニヤ
WHAT'S THE BIG DEAL?
YAAAAAUGH!
Ha ha!
IF YOU GET EMBARRASSED THIS EASILY, YOU'LL NEVER BE ABLE TO HAVE SEX!
Ha ha ha ha!
THIS IS SICK!

I CAN'T STAND SOMEONE LIKE THAT BEING COACH!
キーン
コーン…
I'M GOING TO QUIT THE CLUB.
WHAT DO YOU MEAN? YOU'RE THE CAPTAIN!
PULL YOURSELF TOGETHER!
WASHING HIS BACK IS THE ELEVENTH GRADERS' JOB! I HAD TO DO IT LAST YEAR.
AND YOU'RE OKAY WITH THAT?
IT'S NOT THAT I'M OKAY WITH IT... I MEAN, I'VE NEVER EVEN WASHED MY OWN FATHER'S BACK. BUT STILL...

I'M GOING TO GO TO THE PRINCIPAL. CAN YOU COME WITH ME?

IT WON'T WORK.

WHY NOT?

THEY'D NEVER LISTEN TO JUST TWO STUDENTS' COMPLAINTS. AND BESIDES, EVEN THE PRINCIPAL WOULDN'T DO ANYTHING TO A HIGHLY-RESPECTED COACH LIKE TODO.

BUT...

MAYBE IF THE WHOLE CLUB COMPLAINS ...

THE WAY THE TENNIS CLUB TRAINS CAN'T CHANGE NOW. NO, IT SHOULDN'T CHANGE.

WE'RE GOING TO BE GOING TO THE INTER-HIGH SOON, SO THIS IS A VERY IMPORTANT TIME FOR THE TEAM. WE CAN'T TELL THEM THAT THEY'RE THE VICTIMS OF SEXUAL HARASSMENT NOW.

HUH?

SUZUKI...

NISHIYAMA ...

DIDN'T I TELL YOU? AS LONG AS YOU DO WHAT THE COACH TELLS YOU, NOTHING WILL GO WRONG.

I TOLD YOU NOT TO STIR UP ANY TROUBLE, RIGHT?

IT'D BE DANGEROUS TO GET THEM ANY MORE RILED UP.

IS THIS WHAT SHE MEANT?

I CAN UNDERSTAND. YOU'RE AN ACE WHO'S REACHING FOR THE TOP.
AND BESIDES...
...YOU WANT TO GO TO THE INTER-HIGH, RIGHT? THAT'S WHY YOU WASHED THE COACH'S BACK, RIGHT?
YOU'RE NOT FOOLISH ENOUGH TO QUIT AND GIVE UP YOUR DREAM OVER A LITTLE THING LIKE THIS, ARE YOU?
ALL RIGHT? YOU JUST HAVE TO HANG IN THERE.

スパーン…
パーン
A LITTLE THING LIKE THIS?
IS IT THE CAPTAIN'S JOB TO PRETEND THAT HE'S NOT SEXUALLY HARASSING THE CLUB MEMBERS?
AM I SUPPOSED TO PROTECT HIS "CUSTOMS"?

EMBARRASSING TECHNIQUES

PRO WRESTLING

プロレス

LISTEN UP! ANY OF YOU WHO DOUBLE FAULT WILL DO THIS!

THE TENSION'S HIGHEST WHEN YOU'RE SERVING, SO YOU HAVE TO PRACTICE DOING IT UNDER PRESSURE!

THERE ARE ONLY TWO WEEKS LEFT UNTIL THE MATCH, BUT YOU GUYS ARE STILL NERVOUS!

GOT IT? NO COMPLAINTS, RIGHT?

I SAW THAT, SATO!

Hey! Get over here!

aaaaugh!

......
WE HAVE TO DO IT TO WIN.
YEAH.
UUUGH, I'M NOT DOING THIS. I'M LEAVING.
TODO'S SEXUAL HARASSMENT IS GETTING WORSE.
BUT I'M THE ONE WHO'S LETTING IT HAPPEN.
You're not gonna get away!
HEH HEH. GOT YA.
GAH!
HUH? KUNIYASU?

ドカッ
......

AAAUGH! COACH!
ザワザワ
COACH TODO IS SEXUALLY HARASSING YOU?
INDECENT CONDUCT?
PRINCIPAL'S OFFICE
WHAT ARE YOU TALKING ABOUT, KUNIYASU? YOU'RE EXAGGERATING!
NO, I'M NOT! EVERYONE IN THE CLUB HATES WHAT HE DOES!
EVERYONE IN THE CLUB? YOU MEAN HE WAS JUST PENALIZING THEM A LITTLE FOR SOMETHING THEY DID WRONG?

COACH TODO WAS JUST TRYING TO MAKE YOU STRONGER, RIGHT? HE DIDN'T BEAT YOU OR HIT YOU, RIGHT?
YOUR WATER, SIR.
YOU CALL SPREADING A WOMAN'S LEGS JUST "A LITTLE" PUNISHMENT?
IF THAT'S THE CASE...
Hmm...
IT WASN'T PHYSICAL PUNISHMENT, SO...
HEY! WAIT A MINUTE HERE!
IS SEXUAL HARASSMENT ONLY A PROBLEM WHEN IT INVOLVES PHYSICAL BEATING?
SO YOU'RE JUST GOING TO LET HIM EMBARRASS ALL OF THE CLUB MEMBERS?
WATCH YOUR MOUTH, KUNIYASU.
Let me go! Get Coach Todo here!
......
THIS STUDENT IS ALWAYS LIKE THIS.

SHE'S A FAR CRY FROM THE TYPE OF GIRL WHO DOESN'T SAY "NO" AND THEN CRIES HERSELF TO SLEEP OVER WHAT HAPPENS.
THERE WASN'T A SINGLE TEACHER WHO LISTENED TO HER.
INSTEAD, THEY ONLY SAW HER AS A STUDENT WHO KICKED A TEACHER, AND BEGAN CONSIDERING HER EXPULSION.
TENNIS CLUB
BOYCOTT? ALL OF US?
YES, UNTIL THEY REALIZ WE REALLY HAVE BEEN SEXUALLY HARASSED!
WE HAVE TO PROVE TO THEM THAT WHAT KUNIYASU SAID WASN'T A LIE.
You'll do it, right, Emi? Eriko?
Y...YEAH.
IT'S OKAY FOR YOU, SUZUKI. YOU'RE STILL IN ELEVENTH GRADE.
HUH?

BUT I'M A SENIOR. IF I GO AGAINST THE COACH, I'LL NEVER GET SCOUTED BY A COLLEGE.
ESPECIALLY NISHIYAMA. SHE NEEDS TODO'S RECOMMENDATION FOR A COLLEGE.
Me neither.
......
SORRY, BUT THE SENIORS ARE GOING TO PASS ON THE BOYCOTT.
HUH? IT'S DANGEROUS FOR US ELEVENTH GRADERS, TOO!
ザワザワ
TODO'S MY P.E. TEACHER, AND I'M AT THE TOP OF THE CLASS.
AND I'M JUST A FRESHMAN.
BESIDES, YOU ALREADY HAVE A LOT OF PEOPLE.
SO IT'S JUST GOING TO BE US? SCARY! IF ALL OF THE CLUB MEMBERS WERE WITH US, THAT'D BE OKAY, BUT NOW...
SO SHOULD WE GET THE SIGNATURES?

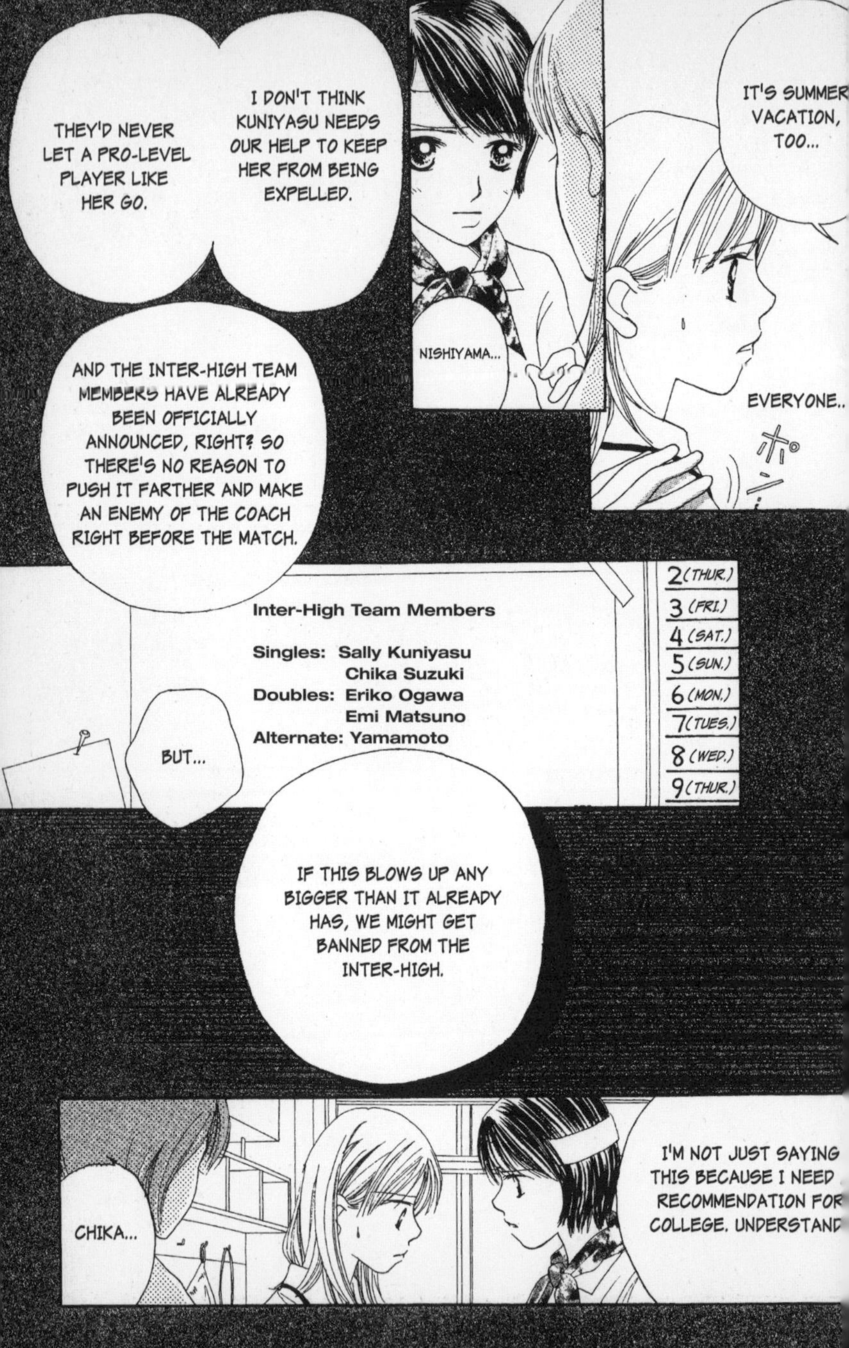
IT'S SUMMER VACATION, TOO...
EVERYONE..
NISHIYAMA...
I DON'T THINK KUNIYASU NEEDS OUR HELP TO KEEP HER FROM BEING EXPELLED.
THEY'D NEVER LET A PRO-LEVEL PLAYER LIKE HER GO.
AND THE INTER-HIGH TEAM MEMBERS HAVE ALREADY BEEN OFFICIALLY ANNOUNCED, RIGHT? SO THERE'S NO REASON TO PUSH IT FARTHER AND MAKE AN ENEMY OF THE COACH RIGHT BEFORE THE MATCH.
2 (THUR.)
3 (FRI.)
4 (SAT.)
5 (SUN.)
6 (MON.)
7 (TUES.)
8 (WED.)
9 (THUR.)
Inter-High Team Members
Singles: Sally Kuniyasu
Chika Suzuki
Doubles: Eriko Ogawa
Emi Matsuno
Alternate: Yamamoto
BUT...
IF THIS BLOWS UP ANY BIGGER THAN IT ALREADY HAS, WE MIGHT GET BANNED FROM THE INTER-HIGH.
I'M NOT JUST SAYING THIS BECAUSE I NEED RECOMMENDATION FOR COLLEGE. UNDERSTAND
CHIKA...

THIS IS PROBABLY GOING TO BE THE FIRST AND LAST CHANCE FOR ME TO GO TO THE INTER-HIGH. FOR YOU, TOO, CHIKA. THAT'S WHY I'VE BEEN TRAINING SO HARD EVERY DAY.
ME TOO. I'M JUST THE ALTERNATE, BUT I'M REALLY HAPPY TO GO.
AND I'M PROUD JUST TO BE ABLE TO BE THERE TO CHEER YOU ON.
I DON'T WANT TO QUIT THE CLUB EITHER!
MY PARENTS TOLD ME I COULDN'T GO TO A PRIVATE SCHOOL. THEY ONLY LET ME COME HERE BECAUSE I PROMISED THEM I'D BE IN THE CLUB FOR ALL THREE YEARS.
Waaah!
Waah! Waah!
Oh no! What's wrong?
AKO, YOU WERE ONLY PATTED ON THE BUTT, RIGHT?
NO!
IF I TOLD MY MOM I WAS SEXUALLY HARASSED, IT'D MAKE HER CRY.
I DON'T WANT TO TELL HER ABOUT IT, EVEN IF I DIE.

THUMP THUMP
ドクン ドクン
ALL OF US WERE HARASSED AT THE CAMP. BUT THAT'S NOT ALL, IS IT?
THERE'S MORE TO IT THAN THAT...
IS HE DOING SOMETHING TO HER SHE CAN'T TELL ANYONE ABOUT?
THE ODDS ARE AGAINST US.
EVEN IF EVERYTHING'S EXPOSED, IT DOESN'T MEAN THINGS WILL WORK OUT.
EVEN IF WE TELL THEM WE'VE BEEN SEXUALLY HARASSED, THEY'RE NOT GOING TO BELIEVE US.

ALL WE CAN DO IS TRY TO GET THROUGH IT.
YOU SHOULD JUST TRY TO DEAL WITH IT.
That's right! Don't forget to stretch!
One! Two!
STRETCH IT OUT AND HOLD IT FOR TWENTY TO THIRTY SECONDS.
つかつか
AAH, NO, SUZUKI!
LIKE THIS!

RELAX YOUR LEGS.
One! Two!
いーちにー
One! Two!
いーちにー
One! Two!
!
YOU SHOULD JUST TRY TO DEAL WITH IT.

IT'S A STRETCH. JUST A SIMPLE STRETCH.

UNNECESSARY TOUCHING, DIRTY JOKES, AND A LEWD WAY OF TALKING...

IT'S DEFINITELY SEXUAL HARASSMENT.

BUT WHEN WE TRY TO CONFRONT HIM WITH IT, WE'RE AT A DISADVANTAGE BECAUSE HE'S THE COACH, AND WE'RE JUST STUDENTS.

IN A SUPERIOR/INFERIOR RELATIONSHIP LIKE COACH/STUDENT, SEXUAL HARASSMENT CAN GO ON FOR A LONG TIME...

AND IT'S EVEN MORE EMBARRASSING TO TRY TO TELL PEOPLE ABOUT IT.

JUST REMEMBERING IT MAKES ME WANT TO THROW UP.
THAT WAS JUST LIKE...
I HAD TO GET OFF THE BUS BEFORE I GOT TO THE STATION. I GUESS I'LL WALK THE REST OF THE WAY.
THE BREEZE FEELS GOOD.
I DIDN'T KNOW THERE WAS A TENNIS SCHOOL HERE.
OH...

KUNIYASU!

THEY CAN'T KEEP KUNIYASU OUT OF SCHOOL FOREVER.
WHAT'S GOING TO HAPPEN NOW?
THE MATCH IS NEXT WEEK, ISN'T IT?
FACULTY LOUNGE
SUGIYAMA'S REALLY ANGRY...
AND THE PRINCIPAL'S UPSET.
THEY'RE PROBABLY GOING TO EXPEL HER.
HMPF.
IT'S ONLY A MATTER OF TIME BEFORE KUNIYASU APOLOGIZES.
ARE YOU GOING TO LET THAT HAPPEN, COACH TODO? WITHOUT YOUR ACE PLAYER...

YOU'RE RIGHT. KUNIYASU WOULDN'T WANT TO GET EXPELLED.
MORE THAN THAT, SHE WOULDN'T WANT TO GIVE UP BEING IN THE INTER-HIGH.
SHE'LL COME, SHE'LL COME. SHE'LL COME CRYING.
TODO THINKS HE HAS ALL OF THE STUDENTS UNDER CONTROL. HE THINKS EVERYTHING'S GOING TO TURN OUT JUST THE WAY HE WANTS IT TO.
HE'S WRONG.
KUNIYASU ISN'T GOING TO COME.
NOT HER.
HE CALLS THAT KIND OF TRAINING "NECESSARY" FOR THE INTER-HIGH?
HA HA!
THEN I DON'T WANT TO BE IN IT.
KUNIYASU...
WOULDN'T YOU REGRET IT?
HUH? REGRET? I'D REGRET PUTTING UP WITH THAT EVEN MORE.
DON'T MAKE ME LAUGH.
WHAT ABOUT YOU? CAN YOU REALLY PUT UP WITH THE WAY THINGS ARE NOW? ARE YOU REALLY HAVING FUN?
IF IT COMES DOWN TO IT, WOULD YOU EVEN HAVE SEX WITH HIM?

UGH. NOW I'VE GOT KIDS MAKIN' RIDICULOUS ACCUSATIONS AGAINST ME, TOO!
I'M GETTING SICK OF THEM.
NONE OF THE OTHER CLUB MEMBERS COMPLAINED.
THEY STARTED SPREADING RUMORS THAT YOU'RE ENGAGED, THOUGH, COACH TODO.
THAT WASN'T VERY FUNNY.
MAYBE YOU SHOULD STOP FOR NOW BEFORE THINGS GET TOO OUT OF CONTROL.
YEAH, GIRLS THESE DAYS ARE JUST TOO SCARY!
You're popular, so you need to be careful!
WHAT...WHAT ARE THESE GUYS SAYING?!
THEY DID THE SAME KINDS OF THINGS TODO DID?
ARE ALL OF THE MALE TEACHERS IN THIS SCHOOL LIKE THIS?

AM I SUPPOSED TO PUT UP WITH THOSE KINDS OF MEN UNTIL I GRADUATE?
AM I SUPPOSED TO JUST LAUGH IT OFF WHENEVER TODO SEXUALLY HARASSES ME?
I DON'T EVER WANT TO BE THAT KIND OF WOMAN!
ガタッ
I MIGHT REGRET MISSING MY CHANCE AT THE INTER-HIGH, BUT I'D REGRET NOT DOING ANYTHING ABOUT THIS SEXUAL HARASSMENT EVEN MORE FOR THE REST OF MY LIFE.

FACULTY LOUNGE

YOU'RE SAYING THAT COACH TODO SEXUALLY HARASSED YOU?
YES.
AND WHEN I HIT MY CHEST, HE USED IT AS AN EXCUSE TO MAKE ME TAKE OFF MY SHIRT AND BRA.
IF YOU GET EMBARRASSED THIS EASILY, YOU'LL NEVER BE ABLE TO HAVE SEX!
AND THAT TIME IN THE BATHROOM, I THINK HE LET HIS TOWEL DROP ON PURPOSE.
THE PERVERTED THINGS HE SAYS. ALL OF IT.
WASHING HIS BACK.
THE MASSAGE.

IT'S THE TRUT THERE WAS A WITNESS!
WITNESS?
MR. HARA! HE WALKED INTO THE ROOM WHILE IT WAS HAPPENING!
UM...
IS THAT TRUE? WAS SHE NAKED?
Y...YES.
COACH TODO...
YEAH, YEAH.
EVERYTHING SHE SAID WAS TRUE.

YEAH, I ASKED HER TO GIVE ME A MASSAGE.
BUT THERE WASN'T ANYTHING INDECENT ABOUT IT.
AND ABOUT HER WASHING MY BACK... WHERE DO YOU GUYS THINK WE WERE, IN A SOAP LAND OR SOMETHING?
YOU SURE HAVE WILD IMAGINATIONS.
SHE WAS WEARING HER CLOTHES. AND I TOLD HER SHE DIDN'T HAVE TO DO IT IF SHE DIDN'T WANT TO.
Oooh...
Hmm...
AND BESIDES, THE ONLY REASON I ASKED HER TO TAKE HER SHIRT AND BRA OFF WAS SO I COULD MAKE SURE SHE WASN'T HURT.
JEEZ.
THINK ABOUT IT. WOULD I TRY TO DO SOMETHING IN SCHOOL THAT WOULD GET ME FIRED?
IF I REALLY WANTED TO PLAY DOCTOR, THERE ARE OTHER PLACES I COULD GO FOR THAT.
Hmpf. "Other places."
That could be a bit of a problem in itself, but...
Um...
WELL...
WELL, WHY DON'T WE ASK HARA ABOUT IT, SINCE HE'S THE WITNESS.
UH...UMM...

WHAT DID IT LOOK LIKE TO YOU, HARA?
TRY TO REMEMBER.
......
TO BE HONEST, I WAS SHOCKED TO SEE A STUDENT THERE WITH HER SHIRT AND BRA OFF.
BUT THE DOOR WASN'T LOCKED, AND THE WINDOW WAS OPEN...
YEAH, THAT'S RIGHT. AND COACH TODO DIDN'T MOVE A MUSCLE WHEN I CAME IN.
IF HE THOUGHT HE HAD SOMETHING TO HIDE, HE WOULD'VE BEEN RUSHING AROUND TRYING TO COVER IT UP.
I SEE...AND YOU CAN SEE RIGHT INTO THERE FRO THE TEACHERS' LOUNGE, TOO.
HE'D NEVER TRY ANYTHING IN THERE.
AND COACH TODO DOES KNOW ALMOST AS MUCH ABOUT THE BODY AS A DOCTOR...
THAT'S TRUE...
HMPF...
SUZUKI...

COACH TODO WAS REALLY WORRIED ABOUT YOUR WOUNDS.
AND YOU'RE OVERREACTING TO WASHING HIS BACK IN THE BATHROOM. I'M SURE HE WAS MORE EMBARRASSED THAN YOU.
AND WHAT YOU THINK WAS UNNECESSARY TOUCHING WAS PROBABLY JUST HOW HE SHOWS HIS FEELINGS.
I'M SURE HE DIDN'T HAVE ANY ULTERIOR MOTIVES, SO CAN YOU FORGIVE HIM?
EVEN IF HE DIDN'T HAVE ANY ULTERIOR MOTIVES,
I STILL DIDN'T LIKE WHAT HE SAID AND DID!
IT'S HARASSMENT!
SUZUKI, GUYS HAVE THEIR SHARE OF HARDSHIPS, TOO.

HUH?
FOR EXAMPLE, A GUY MIGHT GET ACCUSED OF GROPING A GIRL ON A TRAIN, EVEN IF IT WAS JUST HIS BAG THAT ACCIDENTALLY TOUCHED HER. THEN EVEN IF HE TRIES TO EXPLAIN, NOBODY BELIEVES HIM.
SO HE HAS TO PAY HER A HUGE AMOUNT OF MONEY OR SHE'LL SUE HIM. HAVEN'T YOU HEARD ABOUT THAT? A LOT OF MEN GET FALSELY ACCUSED.
IN SEXUAL HARASSMENT SUITS, THE FEMALE USUALLY WINS. SO GIRLS WILL ACCUSE GUYS OF SEXUAL HARASSMENT ANY CHANCE THEY GET. IT'S HARD, IF NOT IMPOSSIBLE, FOR A GUY TO AVOID.
W...WHY ARE WE TALKING ABOUT THIS ALL OF A SUDDEN?
WELL, IT DOESN'T MATTER NOW. I GUESS I'M JUST A GOOD TARGET FOR THE GIRL STUDENTS
sigh
37, SINGLE, A PHYS. ED. TEACHER...IT ALL FITS THE IMAGE OF A DIRTY OLD MAN.
I...
GO EASY ON ME, OKAY? I'M STARTING TO GET SCARED OF THE STUDENTS.

SUZUKI...
YOU'RE THE ONE WHO'S SAYING AND DOING INAPPROPRIATE THINGS.
......
WHOA... WAS THAT SEXUAL HARASSMENT, TOO?
APOLOGIZE TO COACH TODO.
I WANT YOU TO WRITE A LETTER OF APOLOGY WITHIN THE NEXT TWO DAYS. ALL RIGHT?
WHY?
WHY DO I HAVE TO APOLOGIZE?
THEY'RE THE ONES WHO ARE WRONG, AREN'T THEY?
THEY THINK I'M OVERREACTING?
AREN'T THEY?

I AM NOT GOING TO APOLOGIZE.
CHIKA...HURRY UP AND PUT ON YOUR UNIFORM.
AND WRITE THE APOLOGY, TOO, EVEN IF YOU DON'T REALLY MEAN IT. OKAY?
The match is next week.
バタバタバタ
バン
THIS IS BAD!
KUNIYASU WAS JUST EXPELLED!
LOOK! OUT BY THE BACK GATE!
No way! Seriously? You've gotta be kidding me!
HUH?

KUNIYASU.
ザワ
NO WAY... IT'S RIGHT BEFORE THE MATCH AND THEY EXPEL KUNIYASU?
IT'S BECAUSE SHE REFUSED TO WITHDRAW HER ACCUSATIONS OF SEXUAL HARASSMENT!
ザワ
ドクン ドクン
SHE'S NOT BEING EXPELLED. SHE'S TRANSFERRING.

ちら…
YOU HAVEN'T GIVEN ME YOUR LETTER OF APOLOGY YET.
....
HEY, SUZUKI. THERE ARE PLENTY OF OTHER SCHOOLS YOU CAN TRANSFER TO WHERE YOU CAN ENJOY THE CLUBS MORE.
MAYBE YOU SHOULD THINK ABOUT TRANSFERRING.
WE CAN PUT YOU THROUGH THE PROCESS PRETTY QUICKLY.
JUST LIKE KUNIYASU.

WE CAN PUT YOU THROUGH THE PROCESS PRETTY QUICKLY.
JUST LIKE KUNIYASU.
AND WRITE THE APOLOGY, TOO, EVEN IF YOU DON'T REALLY MEAN IT. OKAY?
....
カチャ
HEY, CHIKA.
WOULD YOU LIKE SOME PEACHES?

YOUR AUNT SENT THEM.
SHE SAID SHE'S COMING TO YOUR MATCH TO CHEER YOU ON.
IT'S CLOSE ENOUGH THAT SHE CAN WALK.
AND I BOUGHT YOU A GOOD-LUCK CHARM, TOO.
LOOK!
I CAN'T CHANGE SCHOOLS.
AND...
I CAN'T TELL THEM I'VE BEEN SEXUALLY HARASSED.
IF I TOLD THEM, IT'D END UP HURTING THEM, TOO.
......
キーンコーン

IS EVERYTHING YOU WROTE HERE WHAT YOU REALLY FEEL?
YES.
ALL RIGHT THEN.
WHISPER
Letter of Apology
NOW DON'T CAUSE ANY MORE TROUBLE, OKAY?
Get your feet back on the ground.
NOW GO OUT THERE AND WIN! WE'RE ALL COUNTING ON YOU.
CHIKA, DON'T LOOK SO DEPRESSED.
IT'S ALL OKAY NOW.
TENNIS CLUB

THAT WAS HARD.
HALF OF ME IS RELIEVED, BUT...
...THE OTHER HALF IS MISERABLE.
Letter of Apology
SUZUKI, I'VE DONE NOTHING BUT TRY TO HELP YOU, AND YOU RETURNED THE FAVOR BY ACCUSING ME OF SEXUAL HARASSMENT.
DO YOU UNDERSTAND HOW THAT FEELS?

Sigh!
LOOK, SUZUKI. IF YOU DON'T REALLY MEAN WHAT'S IN THIS LETTER, I DON'T WANT IT.
THIS ISN'T HOW YOU REALLY FEEL, IS IT?
I...I'M SORRY.
UH, I REALLY MEAN IT.
IS THAT TRUE? YOU STILL THINK OF ME AS SOME SORT OF CREEP, DON'T YOU?
YOU STILL THINK I HAD SOME ULTERIOR MOTIVES, DON'T YOU?
NO, OF COURSE NOT...
I'M STILL NOT CONVINCED!
ALL RIGHT. I'M GOING TO SHOW YOU THAT I DON'T HAVE ANY INDECENT FEELINGS TOWARD STUDENTS...
...AND YOU'RE GOING TO SHOW ME THAT YOU REALLY TRUST ME...
...ONCE AND FOR ALL!

DO YOU REMEMBER WHAT HAPPENED THAT DAY?
YOU WERE SITTING HERE WITH YOUR SHIRT OFF.
AND I WAS HERE.
WHY ARE YOU JUST SITTING THERE? TAKE OFF YOUR SHIRT! WE'RE GOING TO DO A RE-ENACTMENT!
WHAT'S WRONG? YOU MEANT EVERYTHING YOU SAID IN THAT LETTER, RIGHT? YOU TRUST ME, RIGHT?
YES, SIR.
ALL RIGHT.
プチ
I TOOK YOUR BRA OFF LIKE THIS TO MAKE SURE YOU WEREN'T INJURED. IS THAT RIGHT?
Y...YES, SIR.

PAY ATTENTION!
THIS IS THE SECOND TIME HE'S SEEN ME. IT'S EMBARRASSING...
DID I TOUCH YOU ANY MORE THAN THIS?
NO, SIR.
WAS CHECKING YOUR INJURIES JUST AN EXCUSE TO GET YOU NAKED?
NO, SIR.
ALL RIGHT.
READ YOUR LETTER OF APOLOGY TO ME, NICE AND LOUD.
HOW MUCH LONGER DO I HAVE TO TAKE THIS?

COACH TODO ALWAYS THINKS ABOUT THE HEALTH OF HIS STUDENTS FIRST...
I WAS JUST OVERREACTING TO WHAT HAPPENED IN THE OFFICE ON JUNE 20TH.
AND WHEN I WASHED HIS BACK, IT WAS OF MY OWN FREE WILL.
I OVERREACTED TO EVERYTHING.
THIS LETTER DOESN'T SAY H I REALLY FEE
THIRTY MORE TIMES!
BUT I'M STARTING TO THINK IT WAS MY FAULT I WAS BEING SEXUALLY HARASSED AGAIN AS I READ IT OVER AND OVER...
ONE MORE TIME!
I'M STARTING TO THINK THAT I'M THE ONE WHO'S WRONG.
ONE MORE TIME!
!

ハァハァ
ゴホ
ALL RIGHT, THAT'S ENOUGH.
NOW IT'S MY TURN TO PROVE TO YOU I DON'T HAVE ANY INDECENT FEELINGS TOWARD MY STUDENTS.
TAKE OFF ALL YOUR CLOTHES.
YES, SIR...
WHERE DID THE DETERMINATION I HAD BEFORE DISAPPEAR TO?
WHY AM I FOLLOWING HIS ORDERS AGAIN?
WHY AM I DOING IT, EVEN THOUGH I KNOW THAT I'LL REGRET IT LATER? WHAT KIND OF WOMAN AM I TURNING INTO?

......
TAKE A LOOK! AM I TURNED ON?
TAKE A GOOD LOOK!
AM I TURNED ON?
N...NO, SIR.

FEEL IT TO MAKE SURE!
ぐい
HOW ABOUT IT? DID IT CHANGE EVEN A LITTLE?
NO, SIR!
NO, SIR!
I DON'T FEEL ANY DESIRE FOR MY STUDENTS! YOU GOT THAT?

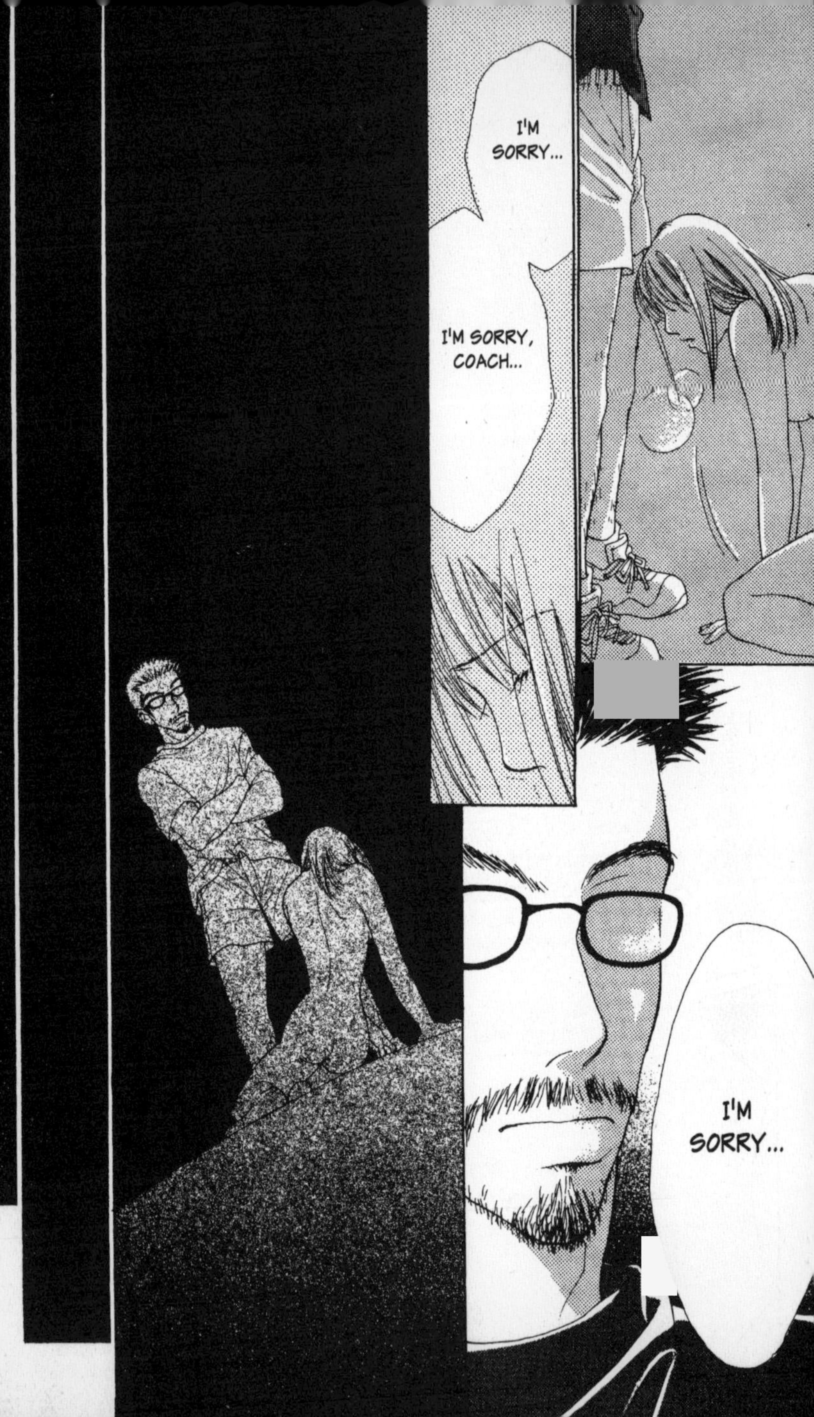
I'M SORRY...
I'M SORRY, COACH...
I'M SORRY...

GAME SET!
IN THIS YEAR'S INTER-HIGH...
...OTOWA SCHOOL FOR GIRLS TIME ON THE COURT WAS VERY BRIEF.
WE WERE CRUSHED IN BOTH THE INDIVIDUAL AND TEAM RANKINGS.

WE CAN'T FORCE HER TO EAT.
SHE'S PROBABLY SHOCKED THAT SHE WASN'T EVEN IN THE TOP EIGHT.
BUT SHE'S BEEN ACTING A LITTLE STRANGE EVER SINCE JUNE...
シャカ シャカ シャカ シャカ
?
......
ばっ

シャカシャカシャカ
YOU SHOULDN'T PLAY THIS SO LOUD.
IT'LL RUIN YOUR EARS.
IT HELPS ME CLEAR MY HEAD.
I'M GOING TO TURN IT OFF, OKAY?
Your desk is such a mess!
WHAT'S THIS?
OH, NO!
...checking my wounds,
Coach Todo XXXXX
just a massage
overreacted
Coach Todo XXXXX
I'm so sorry

LETTER OF APOLOGY? WHAT DID YOU DO, CHIKA?
MASSAGE? NAKED? WHAT'S THIS ALL ABOUT?
IT'S NOTHING, REALLY!
BUT IT'S DEFINITELY YOUR WRITING...
DID COACH TODO DO THESE THINGS TO YOU?
ビリ ビリ
WHAT ARE YOU SAYING? OF COURSE NOT. HE'S A FAMOUS COACH. YOU KNOW THAT, MOM.
TELL ME THE TRUTH, CHIKA.
HE'S AN AMAZING PERSON. HE'S NEVER WRONG, SO, SO...
I NEED TO CLEAR MY HEAD.
I DON'T WANT TO REMEMBER.

CHIKA!
I MADE A BIG FUSS OVER SOMETHING THAT WAS NO BIG DEAL.
YEAH, I'M A VIRGIN, SO I'M JUST NOT USED TO GUYS...
SO...
......

AAAAAAUGH!

so sorry...
...I...
...camp
SHE'S CRIED HERSELF TO SLEEP.
WELL, WE'RE GOING TO HAVE TO MAKE HER QUIT THE CLUB.
OF COURSE.
DAMMIT. I CAN'T BELIEVE HE WAS DOING THAT TO HER.
AND EVEN GOT HER NAKED!
I AM NEVER GOING TO FORGIVE HIM FOR THIS.
I'M GOING.
WHERE'S HIS HOUSE? BRING ME THE SCHOOL DIRECTORY!
HONEY!
CHIKA TOLD YOU NOT TO DO ANYTHING!
AREN'T YOU UPSET ABOUT THIS?
OF COURSE I AM! BUT...
DAMMIT!
BUT...

AUGUST
SUN MON TUE WED
5 6 7 8
12 13 14 15
19 20 21 22
26 27 28 29 30
BEEP
CHIKA, THIS IS EMI.
YOU HAVEN'T COME TO THE CLUB IN A WHILE, SO WE WERE ALL WORRIED ABOUT YOU...
BEEP
THIS IS ERIKO. TODO PICKED ME TO BE THE NEW CAPTAIN TODAY...
I DON'T KNOW IF I SHOULD DO IT, BUT... I DON'T WANT YOU TO PUSH YOURSELF EITHER. I'LL BE FINE.
......
CLICK
ERIKO...
EMI...

EVERYONE...
ARE YOU REALLY OKAY WITH THIS?
BUT...
I KNOW. GOING PUBLIC WITH THIS AND SUING WOULD HURT CHIKA.
BUT, EVEN IF CHIKA QUITS SCHOOL, IT STILL WOULDN'T HELP HER HEAL EMOTIONALLY. I THINK THIS IS THE BEST WAY TO SETTLE THINGS, FOR CHIKA'S SAKE.
......
CHIKA...
コン
コン
CAN I COME IN?
ミーン
ミーン
ミーン

Hey! Ogawa! Murano!
IF YOU HIT A LOB RETURN, YOU NEED TO MOVE FORWARD RIGHT AWAY!
ATTACK SO YOU CAN VOLLEY THE NEXT BALL!
YES, SIR.
GOT IT, OGAWA? YOU NEED COURAGE! COURAGE!
バ"バ"
COURAGE!
ぎゅうっ

EVEN IF HE DIDN'T HAVE SOME ULTERIOR MOTIVE...
THE FACT THAT HE DOESN'T EVEN REALIZE HE'S HURTING ALL THESE GIRLS WOULD MAKE THE PROBLEM JUST THAT MUCH BIGGER.
YOU'RE FRESHMEN, TOO, RIGHT?
COURAGE!
....
YAAAAGH!
DON'T RUN AWAY FROM ME!
BUT THAT'S NOT THE CASE. NO MATTER HOW I LOOK AT IT...
...I JUST CAN'T BELIEVE THAT HE ISN'T EVEN AWARE OF WHAT HE'S DOING.

ANYONE WHO COMPLAINS ABOUT SEXUAL HARASSMENT IS BANISHED.

AND HE USES THAT PERSON AS AN EXAMPLE TO THE OTHER MEMBERS TO KEEP THEIR MOUTHS SHUT.

HE KNOWS THE CLUB MEMBERS DREAM OF GOING TO THE INTER-HIGH, AND USES THAT TO HIS ADVANTAGE TO DO WHATEVER HE WANTS.

BUT THE OTHER TEACHERS JUST SAY, "OH, THE TENNIS CLUB IS ALWAYS INTENSE," AND "THE MEMBERS TRUST THE COACH."

IF THIS CONTINUES, NEXT YEAR MORE FRESHMEN ARE GOING TO COME HERE WITHOUT KNOWING WHAT'S REALLY GOING ON, AND THE SAME THING WILL HAPPEN TO THEM.

TODO'S NOT GOING TO CHANGE. HE'LL JUST KEEP DOING THIS YEAR AFTER YEAR.

ガチャ
CHIKA! WHERE DID YOU GO, WITHOUT TELLING US?
CHIKA?
DAD, MOM...
I...

...I WANT TO TRY TALKING TO THE COACH AGAIN.
HUH?
I WANT HIM TO ADMIT TO COMMITTING SEXUAL HARASSMENT.
I WANT HIM TO APOLOGIZE TO ME AND THE REST OF THE STUDENTS.
IF I DON'T SAY ANYTHING AND JUST QUIT SCHOOL...
...EVERYONE WILL DISMISS IT AS NOTHING, AND HE'LL JUST KEEP DOING IT. I DON'T WANT THAT.
CHIKA...
I CAN'T STAND BACK AND LET IT GO ON...
NOT AS THE CAPTAIN...
...BUT AS A WOMAN.
IS THAT CHIKA?
ザワ
ザワ
WHAT'S GOING ON?
AND HER PARENTS ARE WITH HER.
OTOWA ALL-GIRLS HIGH SCHOOL

ガラッ
FACULTY LOUNGE
HUH?
MR. MATSUOKA.
PRINCIPAL.
COACH TODO.
MY DAUGHTER IS THE VICTIM OF SEXUAL HARASSMENT FROM COACH TODO.
I'D LIKE TO HAVE A WORD WITH YOU.

CONFERENCE ROOM
WE WERE JUST ABOUT TO HAVE THE OPENING CEREMONIES.
JEEZ.
AND THIS HAS ALREADY BEEN DEALT WITH BEFORE.
Sigh... The opening ceremonies...
THIS IS SERIOUS, COACH TODO.
COACH TODO DIDN'T FORCE HER TO COME TO THE OFFICE OR TAKE HER CLOTHES OFF.
PHEW PHEW
BUT MR. SUZUKI...
AND IF IT MADE HER FEEL THAT UNCOMFORTABLE, SHE COULD'VE YELLED OUT OR RUN AWAY.
WHY BRING IT UP NOW?
......
I DON'T BELIEVE MY EARS! I CAN'T BELIEVE THERE ARE PEOPLE WHO CAN SAY THINGS LIKE THAT WITH A STRAIGHT FACE!
WHA?
I SEE NOW... THE REASON THIS SEXUAL HARASSMENT HAS BEEN KEPT QUIET...
...IS BECAUSE YOU'RE ALL DOING THE SAME THING, ISN'T IT?

RIDICULOUS! WE CARE ABOUT OUR STUDENTS!
NONE OF YOU EVEN LISTENED TO MY DAUGHTER WHEN SHE WAS BRAVE ENOUGH TO COME FORWARD...
...OR WHEN YOU WERE GOING TO HAVE THAT OTHER STUDENT EXPELLED.
WHEN A TEACHER ASKS A STUDENT TO DO SOMETHING THAT MIGHT BE EMBARRASSING, HE SHOULD RESPECT HER MODESTY, NOT JUST SAY, "OH, IF SHE SAID SHE DIDN'T LIKE IT, I WOULD'VE STOPPED."
YOU SEEM TO THINK THAT SEXUAL HARASSMENT ONLY BECOMES A PROBLEM WHEN IT INVOLVES PHYSICAL BEATING. BUT ISN'T IT YOUR RESPONSIBILITY TO HELP PROTECT YOUR STUDENTS FROM SEXUAL HARASSMENT EVEN BEFORE IT GETS TO THE POINT OF VIOLENCE?
I AM SURE YOU GENTLEMEN ARE AWARE OF WHAT'S WRITTEN IN THE ARTICLES OF THE CONVENTION OF THE RIGHTS OF THE CHILD?*
......

* CONVENTION OF THE RIGHTS OF THE CHILD, ARTICLE 19: PARTIES SHALL TAKE ALL APPROPRIATE LEGISLATIVE, ADMINISTRATIVE, SOCIAL AND EDUCATIONAL MEASURES TO PROTECT THE CHILD FROM ALL FORMS OF PHYSICAL OR MENTAL VIOLENCE, INJURY OR ABUSE, NEGLECT OR NEGLIGENT TREATMENT, MALTREATMENT OR EXPLOITATION, INCLUDING SEXUAL ABUSE, WHILE IN THE CARE OF PARENT(S), LEGAL GUARDIAN(S) OR ANY OTHER PERSON WHO CONTROLS THE CARE OF THE CHILD.

ばんっ
YOU CAN'T USE THE EXCUSE THAT IT WAS A PART OF YOUR COACHING TECHNIQUE ANYMORE, COACH TODO.
BY HURTING MY DAUGHTER PHYSICALLY AND MENTALLY, YOU'VE VIOLATED HER DIGNITY AS A HUMAN BEING, AND YOU NEED TO APOLOGIZE FOR THAT.
AND WHAT IF I DON'T?
WOULD YOU APPEAL TO THE BOARD OF EDUCATION?
....
NO. NOT THE BOARD OF EDUCATION...
THE BOARD OF EDUCATION WOULD BELIEVE EVERYTHING THE PRINCIPAL'S REPORT WOULD SAY, AND PROBABLY DECIDE TO DEAL WITH IT INTERNALLY...
WE'RE GOING TO TAKE THIS TO CIVIL COURT INSTEAD, SO THAT THE ILLEGALITY OF WHAT YOU'VE DONE, AND THE RESPONSIBILITY OF THE TEACHERS AND THE SCHOOL, IS PERFECTLY CLEAR.
WE ARE ALSO CONSIDERING TAKING THIS TO THE POLICE AND PUBLIC PROSECUTOR'S OFFICE AS A CRIMINAL CASE.
ザワッ
YOU...YOU'D BLOW IT THAT MUCH OUT OF PROPORTION?

YOU THINK I'M BLOWING IT OUT OF PROPORTION?
SLANDER, COERCION, DEFAMATION, INDECENT ASSAULT...
WHAT COACH TODO DID WAS CRIMINAL!
BUT IF IT GOES TO TRIAL, WOULDN'T IT HURT THE GIRL MORE THAN ANYONE ELSE? I CAN'T BELIEVE YOU'D DO THAT TO YOUR OWN DAUGHTER.
MY DAUGHTER IS PREPARED TO DO WHAT IT TAKES!
し……ん…
IF... IF THAT'S THE CASE, THEN WE WON'T JUST SIT BY AND WATCH.
Your water, Principal.
huff huff
I CAN'T BELIEVE THIS IS HAPPENING IN MY SCHOOL.
But it is, so...
COACH TODO!
YOU SHOULD APOLOGIZE, EVEN IF YOU DON'T REALLY MEAN IT.
......
I UNDERSTAND...

IT SEEMS THERE WAS SOMETHING WRONG ABOUT THE WAY I DID THINGS.
AND I ENDED UP COERCING YOU...
I REGRET THAT.
MAYBE I SHOULD'VE ASKED YOU TO DO THOSE THINGS INSTEAD?
cough, cough
COACH TODO...
Ha ha ha ha ha!
WAIT, MR. SUZUKI!
I'LL PUNISH MR. TODO WITHIN THE NEXT COUPLE OF DAYS!
I PROMISE.
Just don't call the police.
I'LL MAKE SURE HIS PUNISHMENT IS SEVERE!
SO...
TODO...

I DON'T KNOW ABOUT THE CONVENTION OF THE RIGHTS OF THE CHILDREN.
You were kind of cool, dad.
Heh heh!
I'M SORRY I SAID YOU WERE PREPARED TO TAKE IT TO COURT WITHOUT ASKING YOU.
IF YOU DON'T WANT TO, I'M NOT GOING TO FORCE YOU.
NO, I DO.
I NEVER THOUGHT ABOUT IT UNTIL THIS MORNING.
BUT WHEN I SAW HOW HE WAS ACTING, I KNEW I WAS PREPARED...
I COULDN'T LET A MAN LIKE HIM BE A TEACHER...
...MAKING FOOLS OF WOMEN LIKE THAT...
I'M GOING TO DO WHATEVER I CAN.

hmpf
...
IF WHAT SHE SAID ABOUT YOU MAKING HER GET NAKED IS TRUE...
THEN...
I'M SORRY, BUT...
I'M SORRY, TOO...
...ABOUT WHAT'S GOING TO HAPPEN TO THE TENNIS CLUB AFTER I'M GONE.
YOU'RE GOING TO HAVE A LOT LESS APPLICANTS NEXT YEAR.
THIS SCHOOL WON'T BE FAMOUS IN THE TENNIS WORLD ANY MORE.
Groan!
I'VE ALREADY HAD AN OFFER FROM F MURA ALL-GIRLS HIGH SCHOOL.
OH, DON'T WORRY ABOUT ME, PRINCIPAL.
HUH?
F MURA? THAT'S OUR SCHOOL'S ARCH RIVAL...
HA!
YOU DON'T SAY...
....

A PAY CUT? THAT'S IT?
DID YOU THINK WE WERE GOING TO FIRE HIM?
NO, THIS ISN'T ABOUT HOW SEVERE THE PUNISHMENT SHOULD BE. ALL WE'RE ASKING...
...IS FOR COACH TODO TO APOLOGIZE... SINCERELY.
DO YOU HAVE ANY IDEA HOW MUCH HE SHAMED AND HURT MY DAUGHTER?
Now, Mr. Suzuki...
IT'S TIME FOR THE OPENING CEREMONIES. I'M SORRY, WE'LL TALK ABOUT THIS AGAIN SOME OTHER TIME.
HUH?
AGAIN? GIMME A BREAK! THERE'S NOTHING LEFT FOR ME TO TALK ABOUT.

Huff, Huff!
Mr. Principal!
PLEASE! KEEP IT DOWN!
NOTHING LEFT TO TALK ABOUT?!
OOPS!

THAT'S ENOUGH ALREADY!
フルフル
THE SCHOOL TAKES RESPONSIBILITY ONLY FOR WHAT HAPPENS DURING THE SCHOOL SEMESTER, AND ONLY DURING SCHOOL HOURS...
...NOT FOR SOMETHING THAT HAPPENED DURING SUMMER BREAK!
YOU'RE ON YOUR OWN! SEE IF I CARE!

HUH?
Huff, huff!
WE NEED TO GET HIM TO THE NURSE'S OFFICE!
NO, BETTER CALL AN AMBULANCE.
バタ ダンッ バタ
バタ バタ
HEY! WAIT A MINUTE HERE!
HEY...
GRRR...
COACH TODO.

I'LL SEE
YOU IN COURT.

ARE YOU SURE ABOUT THIS, CHIKA?
コクン
BUT IT COULD TAKE A LONG TIME BEFORE THE TRIAL IS OVER.
I'M READY... EVEN IF IT TAKES A YEAR OR MORE!
THE TRIAL CAN GO FORWARD EVEN IF I DON'T ACTUALLY APPEAR IN COURT. OR I CAN JUST APPEAR ON SCREEN SO THEY CAN HIDE MY IDENTITY.
I KNOW IT MIGHT NOT GO WELL, BUT I STILL WANT TO DO IT.

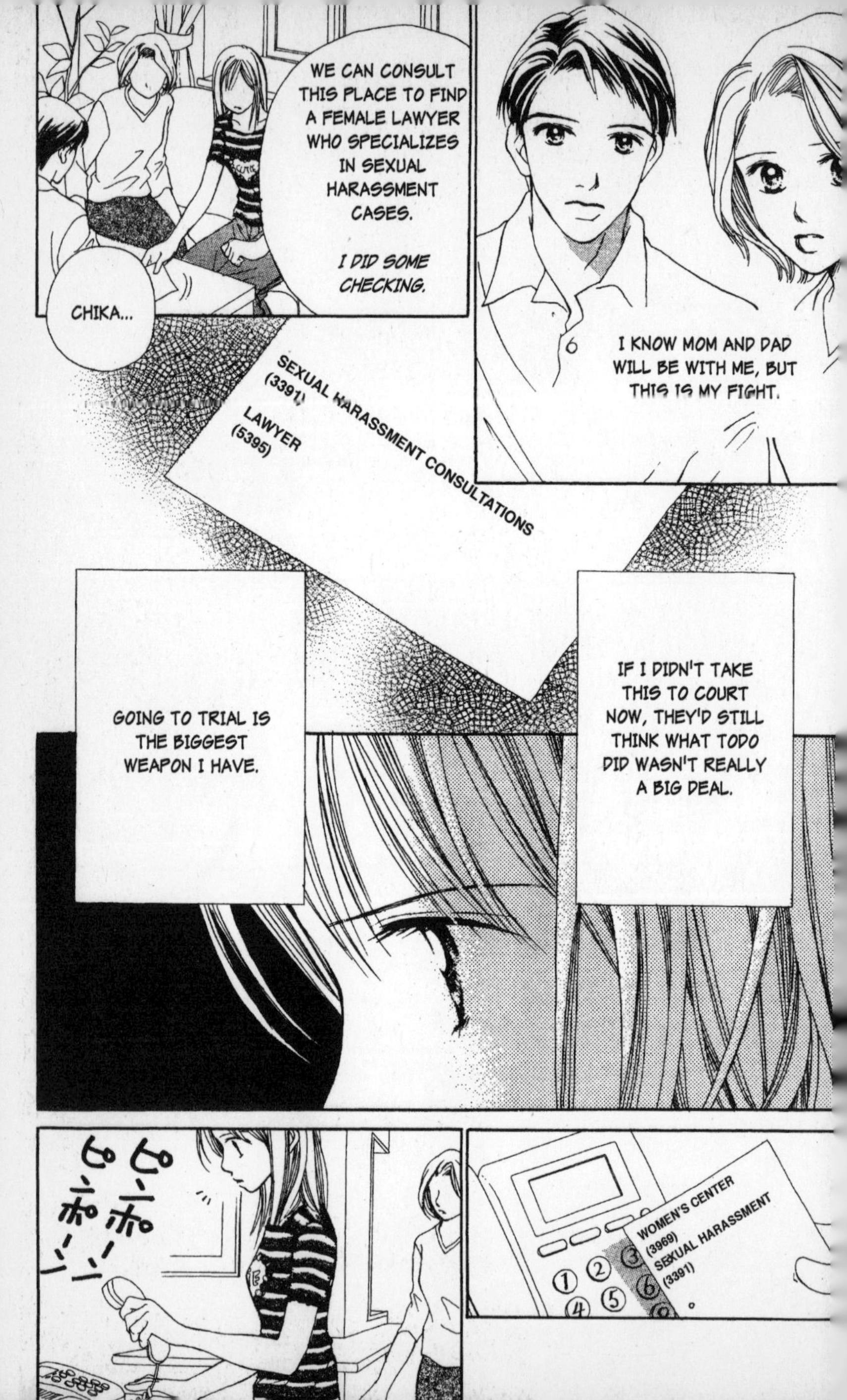

I KNOW MOM AND DAD WILL BE WITH ME, BUT THIS IS MY FIGHT.
WE CAN CONSULT THIS PLACE TO FIND A FEMALE LAWYER WHO SPECIALIZES IN SEXUAL HARASSMENT CASES.
I DID SOME CHECKING.
CHIKA...
SEXUAL HARASSMENT CONSULTATIONS
(3391)
LAWYER
(5395)
IF I DIDN'T TAKE THIS TO COURT NOW, THEY'D STILL THINK WHAT TODO DID WASN'T REALLY A BIG DEAL.
GOING TO TRIAL IS THE BIGGEST WEAPON I HAVE.
WOMEN'S CENTER
(3969)
SEXUAL HARASSMENT
(3391)

CUTIE
EVERYONE ...
ARE YOU SERIOUSLY GOING TO TAKE HIM TO COURT?
I THINK YOU SHOULD GIVE IT UP.

SORRY, BUT NONE OF US CAN TESTIFY FOR YOU.
THE ODDS ARE AGAINST YOU, YOU KNOW.
IF IT GETS OUT TO THE PRESS, IT COULD OPEN THE WAY FOR HUNDREDS OF SUITS AGAINST OTHER SCHOOLS AND PEOPLE. AND EVERYTHING AROUND YOU WOULD COME FALLING DOWN.
I DON'T CARE!
IF THE PRESS LOOKS AT THINGS FROM A WOMAN'S POINT OF VIEW AND TRIES TO FIND THE TRUTH, IT COULD BE A HUGE HELP FOR WOMEN.
THERE'S A CHANCE I CAN WIN.
BUT WHAT I
YOU LOST?
YEAH, CHIKA. IT'D BE HARD FOR YOU TO STAY IN SCHOOL THEN.
AND EVEN IF YOU TRANSFER, WHAT ABOUT THE REST OF US? WE COULDN'T STAY HERE, EITHER.
YOU'D BE MAKING US COMMUTE A LONG WAY TO DIFFERENT SCHOOLS. IS THAT WHAT YOU WANT?

Eriko!

I WILL WIN.

SUZUKI...

IT'S ALREADY GONE FAR ENOUGH.

I REALLY DON'T CARE WHAT HAPPENS BETWEEN YOU AND COACH TODO, BUT NOW THAT YOU'VE MADE THIS BIG OF A FUSS OVER THINGS, THE TEACHERS ARE SO SCARED OF YOU THEY WON'T COME NEAR YOU.

OR ANY OF US.

BUT EVEN IF YOU DO WIN, THERE WILL BE RUMORS GOING AROUND ABOUT ALL OF THE GIRLS IN THE CLUB. PEOPLE WILL BE GOSSIPING ABOUT HOW FAR THEY THINK THE COACH WENT WITH US.

WE'RE GOING TO PRETEND NOTHING EVER HAPPENED.

ARE YOU REALLY GOING T FORGIVE HIM?
BUT HE MUST BE SCARED OF LOSING HIS JOB AND BEING MADE TO LOOK LIKE A CRIMINAL.
HE'S STILL INSISTING THAT WHAT HE DID WASN'T SEXUAL HARASSMENT!
WE HAVE TO MAKE HIM ADMIT IT AND APOLOGIZE!
HE HAS TO PROMISE NOT TO DO IT AGAIN!
CUTIE
AND WE HAVE TO SHOW PEOPLE THAT THE OTHER TEACHERS ARE COMMITTING SEXUAL HARASSMENT, TOO!
ARE YOU TRYING TO CHANGE THE WORLD, CHIKA?
OPEN YOUR EYES AND LOOK AT REALITY!
NEXT WEEK IS THE NEWCOMERS TOURNAMENT! AND DECEMBER IS THE SELECTION TOURNAMENT!

WE'RE PUSHING OURSELVES TO THE LIMITS SO WE CAN MAKE UP FOR LOSING AT THE INTER-HIGH!
TODO'S COACHING IS AMAZING! WE NEED HIM!
....
THEN HOW MUCH ABUSE ARE YOU WILLING TO TAKE FROM HIM?
IT'S NOT LONG BEFORE WE GRADUATE.
IS THIS THE KIND OF WOMAN YOU WANT TO TURN INTO?
DO YOU WANT TO DESTROY THE TENNIS CLUB, CHIKA?
Stop it, you two!
YOU KNOW WHAT EVERYONE'S SAYING, CHIKA?

THEY'RE SAYING THAT IF YOU HADN'T MADE SUCH A BIG DEAL ABOUT SEXUAL HARASSMENT, KUNIYASU WOULDN'T HAVE BEEN EXPELLED.
AND WE WOULD'VE EASILY WON THE INTER-HIGH!
YOU DESTROYED THE BALANCE.
Eriko...
Huff huff
ハア ハア

I...I'M SORRY.
I KNOW YOU'RE RIGHT, CHIKA... I KNOW THAT, BUT...
UGH!
IF WE DID, THEN ALL THAT TIME WE PUT UP WITH HIS SEXUAL HARASSMENT UNTIL NOW AND ALL THAT EFFORT WE PUT INTO OUR TRAINING WOULD'VE BEEN FOR NOTHING.
WE HAD ALL DECIDED TO DO SOMETHING WITH OUR ANGER AND HELP YOU FIGHT.
BUT IN THE END, WE JUST COULDN'T.
IT MIGHT SEEM STUPID, BUT RIGHT NOW, GOING TO NEXT YEAR'S INTER-HIGH IS WHAT'S MOST IMPORTANT FOR US.
PLEASE DON'T CRUSH OUR DREAMS.

......
PUT IT ALL OUT OF YOUR MIND, CHIKA.
NOTHING YOU SAY TO TODO IS GOING TO MAKE A DIFFERENCE.
BESIDES, THAT'S THE WAY MEN HAVE ALWAYS BEEN.
THERE'S NOTHING WE CAN DO ABOUT IT.

カチャ
ジリジリ
WOMEN'S CEN
(3969)
SEXUAL HARAS
CONSULTATION
(3391)
YOU'RE NOT GOING TO TAKE IT TO COURT?
ARE YOU SURE ABOUT THIS?
I'M SURE IF YOU TRIED TALKING TO EVERYONE AGAIN...
DAD...
THE TRIAL ISN'T THE ONLY THING I'VE GIVEN UP ON.

"THAT'S THE WAY MEN HAVE ALWAYS BEEN."
THAT'S WHAT I'VE GIVEN UP ON...
WOMEN ARE...
...THE WEAKER SEX.
...THE OBEDIENT SEX.
...PASSIVE WHEN IT COMES TO SEX.
WHEN I THINK ABOUT IT THAT WAY, EVERYTHING BECOMES SO SIMPLE.
WHEN YOU'RE BORN AS A WOMAN, THERE ARE A LOT OF THINGS YOU JUST CAN'T DO ANYTHING ABOUT.

I'VE GIVEN UP ON MYSELF AS A WOMAN.
SEE YOU LATER.
Huh?
......
"THAT'S THE WAY MEN ARE?" IS SHE GOING TO HAVE TO SPEND THE REST OF HER LIFE BELIEVING SOMETHING SO AWFUL?
SHE THINKS THAT ALL MEN ARE LIKE HIM NOW.
GRRR...
AS A MAN, I...

WE'RE TOO WEAK TO CHANGE ANYTHING, EVEN IF WE TRY.
EVEN IF I WON THE TRIAL, THERE ARE PLENTY OF OTHER GIRLS WHOSE COURT CASES END UP IN PAIN AND HEARTLESS RUMORS.
WOULD I BE CONTENT EVEN IF TODO DID APOLOGIZE TO ME?
PLEASE!
DON'T CRUSH OUR DREAMS.
IF I JUST FORGET ABOUT IT, I CAN GO ON WITH MY LIFE...
IF BEING AT SCHOOL GETS TOO HARD, I CAN JUST QUIT.
IT'S THAT SIMPLE.
SQUISH

OH, NO. THERE'S NOTHING BUT GUYS IN THIS CAR.
HE'S GROPING ME!

I CAN'T SAY ANYTHING.
WHY?
ST...
THAT'S THE WAY MEN ARE.
STOP IT, OLD MAN!

STATION MANAGER
I DIDN'T PUT MY FINGERS UP HER UNDERWEAR!
AND BESIDES, PEOPLE WERE PACKED SO CLOSE IN THERE, YOU GOTTA EXPECT PEOPLE TO BRUSH AGAINST YOU, RIGHT?
She's probably selling herself, anyway.
IT FELT GOOD TO YOU, DIDN'T IT? THAT'S WHY YOU JUST STOOD THERE AND DIDN'T SAY ANYTHING!

IS THE FACT THAT YOU GOT CAUGHT THE ONLY THING THAT'S RUNNING AROUND IN THAT HEAD OF YOURS?
LET ME GO!
DON'T YOU CARE ABOUT THIS GIRL YOU JUST VICTIMIZED?
THE POLICE WILL BE HERE SOON.
HUH? THE POLICE? YOU FORGIVE ME, RIGHT?
......
HOLD ON, I KNOW WHAT YOU WANT.
IS THIS ENOUGH?
I DON'T WANT MY WHOLE LIFE TO GO IN THE CRAPPER OVER A PETTY LITTLE THING LIKE THIS. PLEASE!

PETTY LITTLE THING LIKE THIS...
ドン
YOU THINK IT'S SOME PETTY LITTLE THING?
I'VE HAD IT WITH YOU, OLD MAN. I'M GOING TO REMEMBER YOUR NAME AND FACE FOR THE REST OF MY LIFE.
....

KODAN LINE MAIN ENTRANCE
THANK YOU SO MUCH.
THAT KIND OF STUFF HAPPENS A LOT ON THIS TRAIN.
I WONDER WHAT HAPPENED TO THOSE WOMEN-ONLY CARS THEY WERE SUPPOSED TO HAVE?
I GUESS THIS LINE DOESN'T HAVE ANY OF THOSE THIS TIME OF DAY.
IT DOESN'T MEAN ANYTHING IF THOSE CARS DON'T RUN DURING THE MORNING RUSH HOUR WHEN THEY'RE NEEDED THE MOST.
YEAH, IT IS A PROBLEM.
BUT ANYWAY, I'LL LENGTHEN MY SKIRT AND...
...AVOID THE MORNING RUSH FROM NOW ON.
WHAT ARE YOU TALKING ABOUT?
DOESN'T WHAT HAPPENED BOTHER YOU? YOU'RE JUST GOING TO BRUSH IT OFF?

But...
MY LITTLE SISTER HAS THE SAME THING HAPPEN TO HER EVERY DAY.
AND SHE SAID THE SAME THING AS YOU.
SHE GOT ON THE 6:00 TRAIN THIS MORNING, SAME AS ALWAYS.
IT SEEMS WRONG. THE VICTIM SHOULDN'T HAVE TO JUST TAKE IT AND GIVE UP.
IT'S WRONG.
TRAIN APPROACHING ON TRACK...
プルルルル

SEE YA!
......
DO YOU THINK THEY'LL PUT OUT MORE WOMEN-ONLY CARS?
IF EVERYONE ASKS FOR THEM?
IF WE ALL PUSH FOR THEM?
プシュー
ガタン
ゴトン
ガタン…

I'M SURE...
...THERE ARE TIMES IN LIFE...
...WHEN YOU COULD DO MORE THAN JUST LET IT PASS...
...BUT YOU HAVE TO GIVE UP ANYWAY.

BUT IT'S SAD...
...IF GIVING UP FORCES YOU TO CHANGE YOUR LIFE...
...AND MAKES YOU HATE EVERYONE INVOLVED IN THE SITUATION.
IN THOSE KINDS OF SITUATIONS, YOU SHOULDN'T GIVE IN.
YEAH, I GUESS THAT...
...EVEN THOUGH THERE ARE TIMES IN LIFE YOU HAVE TO GIVE UP...
...THERE ARE ALSO TIMES WHEN YOU JUST CAN'T.

IN OTHER WORDS, THERE ARE TIMES WHEN YOU FEEL, "NO MATTER WHAT, I JUST CAN'T GIVE IN ON THIS ONE THING."
BROADCASTING ROOM

SEXUAL HARASSMENT.
THE WORDS "SEXUAL HARASSMENT" BECAME WIDELY FAMILIAR IN JAPAN IN 1989. IT WAS EVEN PICKED AS ONE OF THE TOP BUZZWORDS OF THAT YEAR.
I RECOGNIZED THE WORDS, BUT I NEVER REALLY THOUGHT ABOUT WHAT THEY REALLY MEANT BEFORE.
Huh?
NOT UNTIL I WAS SEXUALLY HARASSED.
CHIKA?
SEXUAL HARASSMENT IS DIFFERENT FROM PHYSICAL BEATING AND ASSAULT BECAUSE IT CAN BE HIDDEN MORE EASILY.
AND IT DOESN'T LEAVE MUCH EVIDENCE, SO IT'S HARD TO GET IT RECORDED AS A CRIME.
AND NOT ONLY THAT, BUT THERE ARE A LOT OF CASES WHERE THE HARASSER IS IN A MORE POWERFUL POSITION THAN THE VICTIM, SO IT'S EVEN HARDER FOR THE VICTIM TO COME FORWARD.
AND IF SHE DOES COME FORWARD, MEN RIDICULE HER FOR MAKING A HUGE FUSS ABOUT SEXUAL HARASSMENT OVER "SOME STUPID LITTLE THING," OR CALL HER A BITCH.

THERE ARE PEOPLE WHO THINK THAT SEXUAL HARASSMENT ISN'T SUCH A BIG DEAL AND THAT THERE SHOULD BE LAWS ABOUT IT.
BUT LEGALLY, VERBAL SEXUAL HARASSMENT IS SLANDER, AND TOUCHING A WOMAN IN WAYS SHE DOESN'T WANT YOU TO IS INDECENT ASSAULT.
3-A
Everyone, study on your own! I'll be right back!
ドドド
SUZUKI! WHAT IN THE WORLD DO YOU THINK YOU'RE DOING?
OPEN UP!
YEAH, THE ONLY STUDENT WHO WOULD BE GOING ON AND ON ABOUT SEXUAL HARASSMENT IS SUZUKI.
ALL RIGHT THEN, SUZUKI, I HAVE A QUESTION!
SAY YOU GOT TOUCHED ON THE BUTT BY KIMUTAKU. WOULD YOU ACCUSE HIM OF SEXUAL HARASSMENT?
NO.

SO IT'S OKAY FOR KIMURA, BUT NOT FOR AN OLD GUY LIKE ME? THAT'S AN INSULT TO ME AS A MAN!
THE PERSON ON THE RECEIVING END IS THE ONE WHO DECIDES IF IT'S OFFENSIVE TO HER OR NOT. AM I WRONG?
....
I GET IT...
YOU THINK SO? WOMEN HAVE THE RIGHT TO DECIDE FOR THEMSELVES, DON'T THEY?
YEAH! SHE'S RIGHT!
SHH!
I'M TRYING TO LISTEN.
QUIET DOWN! CONTINUE YOUR LESSON!
ザワ ザワ
In short, the penis...
ARE YOU LISTENING, COACH TODO?
CALLING OUT THE NAME OF THE SEXUAL ORGANS OVER AND OVER IS SEXUAL HARASSMENT, TOO.
TELL ME ABOUT IT!
HE'S ALWAYS DOING THAT.

IN THE MIDDLE OF CLASS, COACH TODO ASKED, "YOU'RE STILL A VIRGIN?" AND LAUGHED AT ME. I WAS HUMILIATED!
HE MADE ME WASH HIS BACK AT CAMP. HE MADE ME CLIMB ON HIM TO GIVE HIM A MASSAGE. HE TOOK MY BRA OFF TO "CHECK FOR INJURIES."
IT'S EMBARRASSING, BUT I CAN TALK ABOUT IT NOW.
ME, TOO!
THE COACH MADE ME TAKE OFF ALL OF MY CLOTHES IN FRONT OF HIM.
CHIKA!
Dammit!
COACH TODO MIGHT NOT HAVE BEEN ABLE TO TELL THAT I HATED IT SO MUCH.
BUT MY HEART WAS POUNDING, MY HEAD WENT BLANK... IT WAS ALMOST AS IF MY EMOTIONS HAD BECOME COMPLETELY DETACHED FROM MY BODY.
EVERY TIME I REMEMBERED IT, I WANTED TO THROW UP, AND I COULDN'T SLEEP.

TO THE TEACHERS AND THE PRINCIPAL: DO YOU REALLY BELIEVE THAT "THERE IS NO SEXUAL HARASSMENT GOING ON IN THIS SCHOOL"?
IF THAT'S TRUE, THEN YOU DON'T KNOW ANYTHING ABOUT YOUR STUDENTS, AND YOU'VE NEVER SEEN IT.
AND ISN'T THAT EVEN MORE EMBARRASSING THAN ADMITTING THAT THERE'S SEXUAL HARASSMENT GOING ON?
TO MR. SUGIYAMA, WHO SAID THAT IF I HATED IT THAT MUCH, I COULD'VE YELLED OUT OR RUN AWAY:
WOULD YOU SAY THE SAME THING IF IT WAS YOUR WIFE OR DAUGHTER WHO WAS FORCED TO GET NAKED?
ドドン
SUZUKI! THAT'S ENOUGH!
....
AND TO THE FEMALE TEACHERS... WHY DO YOU COME TO SCHOOL IN SUCH PLAIN, BORING CLOTHES?
IT'S STRANGE THAT YOU WOULD WEAR SUCH PLAIN CLOTHES WHEN WEARING MORE ATTRACTIVE ONES WOULD BE PERFECTLY FINE.
IS IT BECAUSE YOU SUBCONSCIOUSLY KNOW THAT IF YOU WEAR MORE ATTRACTIVE CLOTHES, YOU MIGHT BECOME THE TARGET OF THE MEN'S SEXUAL HARASSMENT?

WHY ARE YOU JUST STANDING THERE? BREAK DOWN THE DOOR!
HURRY!
......
ISN'T IT ABOUT TIME THIS SCHOOL TAKE MEASURES AGAINST SEXUAL HARASSMENT?
SEXUAL HARASSMENT ISN'T JUST SOME LITTLE PROBLEM THAT HAPPENS JUST BETWEEN TWO PEOPLE.
I THINK IT'S JUST AS BIG OF A PROBLEM AS WAR OR MURDER.
DON'T YOU AGREE, EVERYONE?
PEOPLE TALK ABOUT THE EQUALITY OF THE SEXES, BUT WOMEN ARE STILL LOOKED DOWN UPON.
MEN GO AFTER FEMALE STUDENTS AND FEMALE CO-WORKERS THAT HAVE LOWER STATUS THAN THEM BECAUSE THEY MAKE EASY TARGETS. THE MEN KNOW THAT THOSE WOMEN ARE IN A WEAKER POSITION, AND NO MATTER WHAT THE WOMEN TRY TO DO, THE MEN WILL ALWAYS HAVE THE ADVANTAGE.
THAT'S TRUE.
COACH TODO DIDN'T DARE TOUCH THE PRINCIPAL'S DAUGHTER.
......

2-A
QUIET DOWN! TAKE YOUR SEATS!
EVERYONE, IT'S OKAY TO RAISE YOUR VOICES. IF A GUY MAKES UNWANTED SEXUAL ADVANCES TOWARD YOU, THEN THAT'S SEXUAL HARASSMENT.
OGAWA? MATSUNO?
WE WERE SEXUALLY HARASSED, TOO.
SEXUAL HARASSMENT IS A VIOLATION NOT JUST OF YOUR GENDER, BUT OF YOUR ENTIRE LIFE.
It's not just the Tennis Club.
ME, TOO.
ME, TOO.

I THINK THAT HIDING WHAT HAPPENED AND LETTING COACH TODO GET AWAY WITH IT WOULD BE EVEN MORE EMBARRASSING THAN ADMITTING IT!
THERE MIGHT BE GUYS LIKE HIM AT COLLEGE OR WORK.
IF I DON'T DO SOMETHING NOW, I MIGHT BE CRYING MYSELF TO SLEEP OVER SEXUAL HARASSMENT FOR THE REST OF MY LIFE...
...EVEN THOUGH IT'S THE GUY WHO SHOULD BE THROWN OUT OF SOCIETY.
Heeey! Suzuki! Are you trying to threaten me? Or maybe you want money?
......
BUT, EVERYONE...

...WE SHOULDN'T GIVE UP AND SAY, "THAT'S JUST THE WAY ALL GUYS ARE."
IF WE DID, WOULDN'T THAT INCLUDE OUR BOYFRIENDS? OUR FATHERS? OUR BROTHERS?
THAT'S WRONG.
THERE ARE ALSO MEN OUT THERE WHO PROTECT WOMEN.
MEN ARE NOT YOUR ENEMY.

......
SUZUKI.
COACH, I WANT YOU TO DO SOMETHING FOR ME...
Huh?
EVEN IF IT'S JUST FOR A MOMENT, I WANT YOU TO THINK ABOUT HOW THE OTHER PERSON FEELS ABOUT THE THINGS YOU SAY AND DO TO HER.

YOU PROBABLY THINK IT'S NOT SO BAD THAT A WOMAN WOULD CALL IT SEXUAL HARASSMENT.
BUT IF EVEN ONE PERSON IN A HUNDRED DOESN'T LIKE IT, THEN IT *IS* SEXUAL HARASSMENT.
THE PERSON ON THE RECEIVING END IS THE ONE WHO DECIDES IF IT'S OFFENSIVE TO HER OR NOT.

CLAP
CLAP
CLAP
パチ
パチ
CLAP
CLAP
CLAP
パチ
パチ
パチ
CLAP
CLAP
CLAP
パチ
パチ
パチ
パチ
パチ
CLAP
CLAP
CLAP
CLAP
CLAP
CLAP
パチ
パチ
パチ
パチ
CLAP
CLAP
CLAP

パチパチ
パチ
パチ
CLAP
CLAP
CLAP
パチ
パーチパチ
パチ
パチ
パチ
パチ
CLAP
CLAP
CLAP
パチ
パチ
パチ
パチ
パチ
パチ

LATER, COACH TODO ADMITTED THE TRUTH, AND WAS DISMISSED ON CHARGES OF SEXUAL HARASSMENT.

HE DIDN'T APOLOGIZE TO THE STUDENTS UNTIL THE VERY END.

BUT I WANT TO BELIEVE THAT OUR FEELINGS GOT THROUGH TO HIM.

KODAN LINE
I GET GROPED EVERY DAY, TOO!
I CAN'T STAND IT!
AND THEY'RE GETTING EVEN MORE BLATANT! ONE GUY EVEN ASKED IF HE COULD TOUCH ME!
HEY, HEY!
OF COURSE HE CAN'T!

IF SOME GUY TOUCHES ME, I'M GONNA STAB HIM WITH THIS PIN.
IT'LL BE EVIDENCE.
SO HE CAN'T SAY IT WASN'T HIM AND THEN RUN AWAY.
TA-DA!
WHOA, THAT'S BIG!
I ALWAYS HAVE ONE ON MY SKIRT.

I'M NOT GOING TO STAND BY AND BE A VICTIM ANYMORE.
IT'S ACTUALLY A RELIEF TO BE BRAVE AND STAND UP FOR MYSELF.
I FEEL THE SAME WAY!
IT'S LIKE, IF YOU'RE SERIOUS, THINGS WILL START TO CHANGE.
EVERYONE...
THINGS PROBABLY AREN'T GOING TO CHANGE VERY EASILY.
BUT THEY WILL CHANGE SOME DAY, LITTLE BY LITTLE...
YEAH.
Isn't that the station manager?
WE WILL NOT TOLERAT GROPIN
I FEEL KIND OF NERVOUS.
What'll we do if he tells us to go away?
DON'T WORRY! THIS GUY WAS NICE TO ME WHEN I GOT GROPED BEFORE.
REQUEST
STATION MANAGER'S OFFICE
EXCUSE ME.
REQUEST

We request that you expand the use of women-only cars on the Kodan Line to:
Weekdays 7:00 AM - 8:30 AM
5:30 PM - 7:30 PM
....
I GOT THE SAME KIND OF REQUEST JUST YESTERDAY.
HUH?
HA HA!
YEAH, IT WAS THAT BOY FROM BEFORE.
AH, SPEAKING OF WHICH...

THE END

COMING SOON

CONFIDENTIAL CONFESSIONS

VOLUME THREE

Kyoko is a normal high school girl living with the extreme pressure forced upon her by her school and her parents. With no positive adult role models or any support from her peers, she experiments with illegal drugs and eventually falls into a deep addiction. Her parents and friends must now try to break her of the habit and somehow make her realize that there are better things in life than addiction.

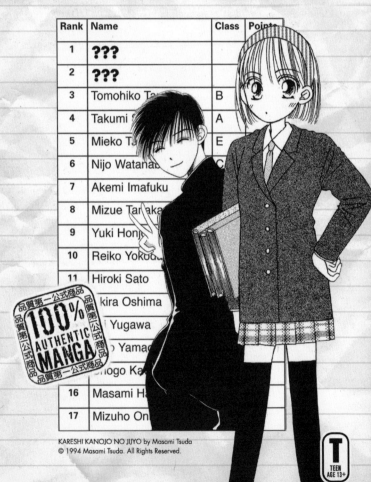

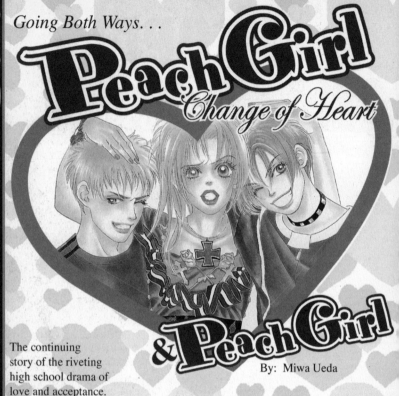

STOP!

This is the back of the book.
You wouldn't want to spoil a great ending!

This book is printed "manga-style," in the authentic Japanese right-to-left format. Since none of the artwork has been flipped or altered, readers get to experience the story just as the creator intended. You've been asking for it, so TOKYOPOP® delivered: authentic, hot-off-the-press, and far more fun!

DIRECTIONS

If this is your first time reading manga-style, here's a quick guide to help you understand how it works.

It's easy... just start in the top right panel and follow the numbers. Have fun, and look for more 100% authentic manga from TOKYOPOP®!